Biblical Women in Crisis

in Crisis

Portraits of Faith and Trust

Biblical Women in Crisis

Portraits of Faith and Trust

Jeanne Kun

The Word Among Us Press
7115 Guilford Drive
Frederick, Maryland 21704
www.wau.org

21 20 19 18 17   1 2 3 4 5

ISBN: 978-1-59325-307-3

Nihil obstat: The Reverend Monsignor Michael Morgan, J.D., J.C.L.
                  Censor Librorum
                  January 25, 2017

Imprimatur: + Most Reverend Felipe J. Estévez, S.T.D.
                  Bishop of St. Augustine
                  January 25, 2017

Scripture passages contained herein are from the New Revised Standard Version Bible: Catholic Edition, copyright ©1989, 1993, Division of Christian Education of the National Council of the Churches of Christ in the United States of America. Used by permission. All rights reserved.

Selections from homilies and addresses by Pope St. John Paul II, Pope Benedict XVI, and Pope Francis are from the Vatican translation and can be found on the Vatican website, www.vatican.va. © Libreria Editrice Vaticana. Used with permission.

Cover Art: "Touch of Faith" by Carolyn Blish
Used with permission
Cover and Text Design: David Crosson

Made and printed in the United States of America
Library of Congress Control Number: 2016957486

Contents

Welcome to
The Word Among Us
Keys to the Bible

Have you ever lost your keys? Everyone seems to have at least one "lost keys" story to tell. Maybe you had to break a window of your house or wait for the auto club to let you into your car. Whatever you had to do probably cost you—in time, energy, money, or all three. Keys are definitely important items to have on hand!

The guides in The Word Among Us Keys to the Bible series are meant to provide you with a handy set of keys that can "unlock" the treasures of the Scriptures for you. Scripture is God's living word. Within its pages we meet the Lord. So as we study and meditate on Scripture and unlock its many treasures, we discover the riches it contains—and in the process, we grow in intimacy with God.

Since 1982, *The Word Among Us* magazine has helped Catholics develop a deeper relationship with the Lord through daily meditations that bring the Scriptures to life. More than ever, Catholics today desire to read and pray with the Scriptures, and many have begun to form small faith-sharing groups to explore the Bible together.

We designed the Keys to the Bible series after conducting a survey among our magazine readers to learn what they wanted in a Catholic Bible study. We found that they were looking for easy-to-understand, faith-filled materials that approach Scripture from a clearly Catholic perspective. Moreover, they wanted a Bible study that shows them how they can apply what they learn from Scripture to their everyday lives. They also asked for sessions that they could complete in an hour or two.

Our goal was to design a simple, easy-to-use Bible study guide that is also challenging and thought provoking. We hope that this guide fulfills those admittedly ambitious goals. We are confident, however, that taking the time to go through this guide—whether by yourself, with a friend, or in a small group—will be a worthwhile endeavor that will bear fruit in your life.

How to Use the Guides in This Series

The study guides in the Keys to the Bible series are divided into six sessions that each deal with a particular aspect of the topic. Before starting the first session, take the time to read the introduction, which sets the stage for the session that follows.

Whether you use this guide for personal reflection and study, as part of a faith-sharing group, or as an aid in your prayer time, be sure to begin each session with prayer. Ask God to open his word to you and to speak to you personally. Read each Scripture passage slowly and carefully. Then, take as much time as you need to meditate on the passage and pursue any thoughts it brings to mind. When you are ready, move on to the accompanying commentary, which offers various insights into the text.

Two sets of questions are included in each session to help you "mine" the Scripture passage and discover its relevance to your life. Those under the heading "Understand!" focus on the text itself and help you grasp what it means. Occasionally a question allows for a variety of answers and is meant to help you explore the passage from several angles. "Grow!" questions are intended to elicit a personal response by helping you examine your life in light of the values and truths that you uncover through your study of the Scripture passage and its setting. Under the headings "Reflect!" and "Act!" we offer suggestions to help you respond concretely to the challenges posed by the passage.

Finally, pertinent quotations from Church Fathers and papal texts and homilies, as well as writings and testimonies of contemporary Christians, appear throughout the sessions. Coupled with relevant information about the history and geography of ancient Palestine, these selections (called "In the Spotlight") add new layers of understanding and insight to your study.

As is true with any learning resource, you will benefit the most from this study by writing your answers to the questions in the spaces provided. The simple act of writing can help you formulate your thoughts more clearly—and will also give you a record of your reflections and spiritual growth that you can return to in the future to see how much God has accomplished in your life. End your reading or study with a prayer thanking God for what you have learned—and ask the Holy Spirit to guide you in living out the call you have been given as a Christian in the world today.

Although the Scripture passages to be studied and the related verses for your reflection are printed in full in each guide (from the New Revised Standard Version Bible: Catholic Edition), you will find it helpful to have a Bible on hand for looking up other passages and cross-references or for comparing different translations.

The format of the guides in The Word Among Us Keys to the Bible series is especially well suited for use in small groups. Some recommendations and practical tips for using this guide in a Bible discussion group are offered on pages 116–119.

We hope that this guide will unlock the meaning of the Scriptures for you. As you become acquainted with the biblical women who are featured in this guide, may you learn from them to respond with faith and trust to crises and hard times that you may encounter in your own life.

Jeanne Kun
The Word Among Us Press

Introduction

Meeting Crises with Faith and Trust

For more than forty-five years, I've been an avid reader of the Bible, and during the course of the past fifteen years, I've written ten Bible study guides on a wide variety of topics and themes. Yet even with such familiarity with Scripture, every time I delve into God's word, I find it amazingly fresh and exciting. With any given day's reading, I might gain a new insight into God's nature and character or grasp one of his truths with greater understanding. Or I might get better acquainted with one of the personalities whom I encounter in the pages of the Old and New Testaments. Most often, it's the women of the Bible who capture my attention. They intrigue and fascinate me.

Over the years I've come to consider numerous women whom I've "met" in the Bible as my good friends. They have served as mentors and guides in many situations in my life. So researching and writing this newest of my contributions to the Keys to the Bible series has been an opportunity for me to renew or deepen several of these friendships and to ponder again the lessons these women have taught me.

Women Facing Challenges or Decisions

So what will we gain from getting to know the women whose lives are presented here before us? What can be learned from observing how they responded to the challenging situations they found themselves in? How are we to approach this guide to get the most out of it, spiritually and practically? The title and subtitle, *Biblical Women in Crisis: Portraits of Faith and Trust*, give us some clues.

Biblical Women. All the women whose lives we'll examine in some depth are *biblical* figures. The Old Testament offers the accounts of the Hebrew midwives Shiphrah and Puah as well as Naomi and Ruth and Hannah. The stories of Jesus' mother, Mary, the woman identified only by her chronic issue of blood, and Martha are brought to us in the New Testament. More particularly, these are women of the Bible who faced grave difficulties and decisive, defining moments in their own lives.

In the supplementary "In the Spotlight" selections in this study guide, we'll also meet several contemporary women and be inspired as we read about how they responded to the challenges presented to them by the modern world.

In Crisis. *The Oxford American Dictionary and Language Guide* defines the word "crisis" as "a time of intense difficulty or danger." It also states that a crisis may be "a time when a difficult or important decision must be made." Synonyms that describe a crisis are "crunch," "dilemma," "trouble," "predicament," and "dire straits." Those relating to crucial decision making are "quandary," "hour of decision," "moment of truth," and "turning point."

We'll observe the Hebrew midwives as they were confronted with the evil and immoral demand of a powerful oppressor. Naomi and Ruth knew the grief of widowhood and the plight of poverty. Hannah suffered not only the empty ache of her infertility but the mockery of her heartless rival, Peninnah. God's unexpected and incredibly life-changing request took the young virgin Mary by surprise. The woman with the hemhorrage endured years of pain, discomfort, and inconvenience, as well as the loss of personal relationships and social standing, all due to a physical disorder on which she had drained her financial resources as she went from doctor to doctor, hoping to be cured. A hospitable but harried hostess, Martha confronted the Lord—and herself—in her struggle to get her priorities straight. These situations could easily fit one of the definitions of "crisis"!

When these biblical women in crisis responded in faith and trust in the Lord, great things happened in their own lives—and for the generations that followed them. Their faith and trust prevailed, and they experienced breakthroughs, miracles, and peace.

Faith in Action

Of course, there are also plenty of ways to define "faith"—"confidence," "conviction," "hope," "certitude," and "assent" are all synonyms. But ultimately, it's the Bible that gives us the best definition, especially in those scenes in the Gospels where Jesus commended people for their belief in him. For example, the Evangelist Matthew tells us of the bold woman who was undeterred and undaunted when she turned to Jesus, sure that he could—and would—help her daughter:

> Just then a Canaanite woman from that region came out and started shouting, "Have mercy on me, Lord, Son of David; my daughter is tormented by a demon." But he did not answer her at all. And his disciples came and urged him, saying, "Send her away, for she keeps shouting after us." He answered, "I was sent only to the lost sheep of the house of Israel." But she came and knelt before him, saying, "Lord, help me." He answered, "It is not fair to take the children's food and throw it to the dogs." She said, "Yes, Lord, yet even the dogs eat the crumbs that fall from their masters' table." Then Jesus answered her, "Woman, great is your faith! Let it be done for you as you wish." And her daughter was healed instantly. (Matthew 15:22-28)

Likewise, the level of trust and confidence in Jesus that another Gentile, a Roman soldier, exhibited was quite striking:

> When he entered Capernaum, a centurion came to him, appealing to him and saying, "Lord, my servant is lying at home paralyzed, in terrible distress." And he said to him, "I will come and cure him." The centurion answered, "Lord, I am not worthy to have you come under my roof; but only speak the word, and my servant will be healed. For I also am a man under authority, with soldiers under me; and I say to one, 'Go,' and he goes, and to another, 'Come,' and he comes, and to my slave, 'Do this,' and

the slave does it." When Jesus heard him, he was amazed and said to those who followed him, "Truly I tell you, in no one in Israel have I found such faith. . . . " And to the centurion Jesus said, "Go; let it be done for you according to your faith." And the servant was healed in that hour. (Matthew 8:5-10, 13)

These are only two depictions of faith among the many stories in the Gospels (for example, see Mark 10:46-52 and Luke 7:44-50). The Old Testament also vividly describes the posture and deeds of faith exhibited by such men and women as Abraham, Moses, Joshua, Deborah, Gideon, Judith, Esther, and David.

Taking a step of faith, putting faith into action, living by faith—each goes hand in hand with having the courage to trust God, to hand over control to God, to "let go and let God." As these popular adages note, "Courage follows when faith takes the lead" and "Courage doesn't come from an absence of fear but an abundance of faith."

Shiphrah and Puah, Naomi and Ruth, Hannah, Mary, the woman with chronic bleeding, and Martha were ordinary women, but women who possessed and acted with an extraordinary amount of faith and courage, which enabled them to overcome their natural fears.

As Relevant and Pertinent as Ever

Though the biblical women we'll soon meet in the following pages of this guide lived in the distant past, their real-life experiences, as well as their lessons in faith, still speak profoundly to us today. The problems they faced are ageless, timeless ones, common to every era and known by every generation.

Facing the unethical or immoral demands of secular society, losing a spouse, relocating to an unfamiliar town, coping with the sadness of infertility, surprised by an unexpected turn of events, suffering years of chronic illness and desperate for healing or a cure, overwhelmed by the daily routine and monotony of cooking and cleaning house or run down by entertaining houseguests—these are the modern-day equivalents of the biblical scenes played out before us in this guide. Thus, as we study the lives of the women featured here, we'll not only sympathize with them, but we'll also find ourselves identifying with them in many ways. It's likely that each of us has experienced—or at some point in our lives will experience—some of the same challenges, fears, hardships, and times of crisis that they did. So let's take heart from their examples of trust and put our faith in the Lord, confident that he will never abandon us.

"A woman is like a tea bag," says an old Irish proverb. "You never know how strong she is until she gets in hot water." The biblical women in this study guide are women of tested and proven faith, women whose strength was shown when they were steeped in hot water. It can rightly be said of each of them, "I kept my faith, even when I said, / 'I am greatly afflicted'" (Psalm 116:10). They stand among the ranks of Sarah, the mother of Moses, Rahab, Deborah, Esther, Elizabeth, Anna, Mary Magdalene, Joanna, Lydia, and countless other women of great faith whose experiences and lives are recorded in the Bible. May they inspire us to "run with perseverance the race that is set before us, looking to Jesus the pioneer and perfecter of our faith" (Hebrews 12:1-2).

Jeanne Kun

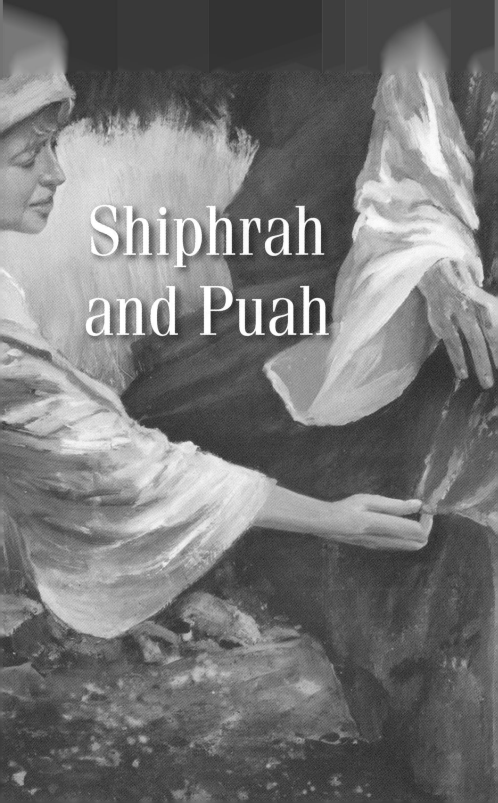

Shiphrah and Puah

Exodus 1:1-22

¹:¹These are the names of the sons of Israel who came to Egypt with Jacob, each with his household: ²Reuben, Simeon, Levi, and Judah, ³Issachar, Zebulun, and Benjamin, ⁴Dan and Naphtali, Gad and Asher. ⁵The total number of people born to Jacob was seventy. Joseph was already in Egypt. ⁶Then Joseph died, and all his brothers, and that whole generation. ⁷But the Israelites were fruitful and prolific; they multiplied and grew exceedingly strong, so that the land was filled with them.

⁸Now a new king arose over Egypt, who did not know Joseph. ⁹He said to his people, "Look, the Israelite people are more numerous and more powerful than we. ¹⁰Come, let us deal shrewdly with them, or they will increase and, in the event of war, join our enemies and fight against us and escape from the land." ¹¹Therefore they set taskmasters over them to oppress them with forced labor. They built supply cities, Pithom and Rameses, for Pharaoh. ¹²But the more they were oppressed, the more they multiplied and spread, so that the Egyptians came to dread the Israelites. ¹³The Egyptians became ruthless in imposing tasks on the Israelites, ¹⁴and made their lives bitter with hard service in mortar and brick and in every kind of field labor. They were ruthless in all the tasks that they imposed on them.

¹⁵The king of Egypt said to the Hebrew midwives, one of whom was named Shiphrah and the other Puah, ¹⁶"When you act as midwives to the Hebrew women, and see them on the birthstool, if it is a boy, kill him; but if it is a girl, she shall live." ¹⁷But the midwives feared God; they did not do as the king of Egypt commanded them, but they let the boys live. ¹⁸So the king of Egypt summoned the midwives and said to them, "Why have you done this, and allowed the boys to live?" ¹⁹The

> Because the Hebrew midwives respected ("feared") God, they knew that the preservation of life took precedence over the murderous decrees of the king, even at the risk of their own lives.
> —Stephen J. Binz, *The God of Freedom and Life: A Commentary on the Book of Exodus*

midwives said to Pharaoh, "Because the Hebrew women are not like the Egyptian women; for they are vigorous and give birth before the midwife comes to them." [20]So God dealt well with the midwives; and the people multiplied and became very strong. [21]And because the midwives feared God, he gave them families. [22]Then Pharaoh commanded all his people, "Every boy that is born to the Hebrews you shall throw into the Nile, but you shall let every girl live."

(See also Exodus 2:1-10.)

Shiphrah and Puah? Not many contestants in a Bible trivia game could identify them! Indeed, the Book of Exodus makes only brief mention of these two women who lived more than three millennia ago. Yet their story is a clarion call to us today to take a stand against sin and wrongdoing, even when the cost of doing so is high.

Exodus tells the story of the deliverance of the "sons of Israel" from their cruel bondage in Egypt. Joseph was the son of the ancient patriarch Jacob. His brothers, who were jealous of him, sold him into slavery, but eventually Joseph rose to great power in Egypt under Pharaoh's authority. So when Jacob and his sons came to Egypt seeking refuge from famine, they were generously welcomed. But life in Egypt did not remain rosy for the Israelite settlers. When a new Egyptian king who did not remember Joseph rose to power (Exodus 1:8), the Israelites endured the bitter oppression that God had foretold to Abraham many generations earlier (Genesis 15:13).

"Pharaoh" is an Egyptian royal title meaning "great house" or "palace." The Book of Exodus never refers to the Egyptian king by a given, personal name. With this impersonal designation and namelessness, we can see in Pharaoh a symbol of the human and spiritual forces that oppressed the Israelites in the time before their "exodus," or departure, from Egypt. It is those same forces that oppress humankind today, but from which Jesus, the Passover Lamb, came to deliver us.

Pharaoh was threatened by the growing strength and number of Israelites in his nation. So when harsh servitude failed as a means of population control (Exodus 1:12), Pharaoh turned to infanticide, ordering that their male newborns be killed (1:15-16). Yet why did he think that the midwives Shiphrah and Puah, women who were dedicated to bring life into the world, would be willing to obey this heinous command to be purveyors of death?

The original Hebrew text of Exodus 1:15 can be translated as "Hebrew midwives" or "midwives to the Hebrews"—both are linguistically possible. Consequently, biblical scholars have debated whether Shiphrah and Puah were Hebrews themselves or Egyptians attending Hebrew women in childbirth. If the midwives were Egyptians, Pharaoh might have assumed that they would be compliant to his plan. However, their names are considered by many linguists to be of Semitic origin, not Egyptian—Shiphrah possibly meaning "beautiful," "fair," or "pleasing" and Puah, "splendid."[1]

> Shiphrah and Puah's story is a clarion call to us today to take a stand against sin and wrongdoing, even when the cost of doing so is high.

The Hebrew text states that the midwives refused to carry out Pharaoh's command because they "feared God" (Exodus 1:17). This statement doesn't seem to refer to their regard for the array of Egyptian deities. Throughout the Bible, "fear of the Lord" describes the reverence, respect, and esteem that one has in acknowledgment of and response to God's goodness and power. It is not dreadful fright but rather awe at God's greatness and love. The psalmist writes that "the friendship of the LORD is for those who fear him, / and he makes his covenant known to them" (Psalm 25:14; see also Psalm 34:10-14). Those who fear the Lord are in right relationship with him.

Motivated by their reverent fear of God, Shiphrah and Puah had the courage to honor and obey him rather than the Egyptian king. These women played a key role in preserving life, risking their own lives by defying Pharaoh's order. When Pharaoh questioned why they had "allowed the boys to live" (Exodus 1:18), they shrewdly asserted that Hebrew women were so "vigorous" that, unlike the Egyptians, they quickly gave birth before a midwife could arrive to attend them (1:19).

Shiphrah and Puah's godly refusal to commit infanticide is perhaps the earliest known example in history of civil disobedience to an evil, oppressive regime. The midwives' stand, perhaps at risk to their own lives, protected the baby boys, allowing the Hebrew people to flourish. God rewarded the women for their righteousness, courage, and "fear" by giving them "families" (Exodus 1:21)—children and descendants to carry on life to future generations.

What are the "take-aways" for us today from this story of Shiphrah and Puah?

- The midwives' position of service and influence was no accident; rather, it enabled them to defend the lives of the male Hebrew babies. This gives us an assurance that even in a crisis, God is always at work to further his purposes and accomplish his will.

- Shiphrah and Puah didn't play a passive role in this crisis; they did not become helpless victims. Revering God, they put their trust in him and acted decisively.

- Shiphrah and Puah are surprisingly contemporary models. The conflict presented to them by the Pharaoh's death-dealing command is still played out today when society confronts us with demands hostile to Christianity. The story of the midwives reminds us that we, too, are threatened by evil, including sin, sickness, war, racism, and death. And like Shiphrah and Puah, we may have to risk our reputation, our security, or even our lives for the sake of others. We can only do that when we put our trust in God, who will never fail to help us.

Not to be thwarted in his murderous intentions by the midwives' refusal, Pharaoh commanded "all his people" to throw every boy born to the Hebrews into the Nile River (Exodus 1:22). Yet there is irony here, as Scripture commentator Stephen J. Binz has noted.

> Each form of oppression portends the eventual triumph of Israel. The midwives, in saving the sons from death, foreshadow the saving activity of God in the Passover. The drowning of the boys in the Nile anticipates the way Pharaoh and his armies will meet their death. The oppressive actions, finally, prepare the way for the story of Moses' birth. (*The God of Freedom and Life*)

Shiphrah and Puah's story is brief, but it records a significant event at the beginning of the long story of the Israelites' deliverance. In the chapters that follow, God raises up Moses as a liberator through whom the Israelites gain freedom from their slavery and oppression in Egypt. Ultimately, this "rescue" story told in the Book of Exodus is our story too, for the work of Moses foreshadows the saving work of Christ that sets each one of us free from the bondages of sin and death.

[1] *In the Bible, the term "Hebrew" is normally used by Israelites when speaking of themselves to foreigners, or is used by foreigners when speaking about Israelites. The Israelites/Hebrews were one of the Semitic peoples of the Middle East, and their language was of Semitic origin.*

Understand!

1. What was the new Pharaoh's attitude toward the Israelites who had earlier found refuge in Egypt and settled there? In what ways did the Egyptians oppress the "foreigners" in the land?

_____

_____

_____

_____

_____

2. Read Matthew 2:1-18. What similarities do you see between Pharaoh's desire to kill newborn Hebrew males and King Herod's massacre of the infants in Bethlehem? What were the fears and aims behind the actions of these rulers? How did God foil and derail the evil intents and deeds of both Pharaoh and Herod and ultimately accomplish our salvation?

_____

_____

_____

_____

_____

3. What do you think motivated and enabled the Hebrew midwives to act so courageously? What character traits of these women are displayed by their actions?

_____

_____

_____

_____

_____

4. What were the immediate consequences of the midwives' action? The longer-range outcome? How did God bless Shiphrah and Puah for the stand they took? What does God's response to the midwives' actions reveal about his nature?

_____

_____

_____

_____

_____

5. Read Exodus 2:1-10. What roles did Moses' mother and sister and the daughter of Pharaoh play in God's further intentions for the Israelites and his plan of salvation for all humankind? In what ways were these women audacious "risk takers" like the midwives?

_____

_____

_____

_____

_____

▶ In the Spotlight
Human Life Is Always a Good

Pope Benedict XVI notes that God's immense love for each of us means that each person deserves to be loved.

"Before I formed you in the womb I knew you, and before you were born I consecrated you," God said to the prophet Jeremiah (1:5). And the psalmist recognizes with gratitude: "You did form my inward parts, you did knit me together in my mother's womb. I praise you, for you are fearful and wonderful. Wonderful are your works! You know me right well" (Psalm 139:13-14).

These words acquire their full, rich meaning when one thinks that God intervenes directly in the creation of the soul of every new human being.

God's love does not differentiate between the newly conceived infant still in his or her mother's womb and the child or young person, or the adult and the elderly person. God does not distinguish between them because he sees an impression of his own image and likeness in each one (Genesis 1:26). He makes no distinctions because he perceives in all of them a reflection of the face of his Only-begotten Son, whom "he chose . . . before the foundation of the world. . . . He destined us in love to be his sons . . . according to the purpose of his will" (Ephesians 1:4-6).

This boundless and almost incomprehensible love of God for the human being reveals the degree to which the human person deserves to be loved in himself, independently of any other consideration—intelligence, beauty, health, youth, integrity, and so forth. In short, human life is always a good, for it "is a manifestation of God in the world, a sign of his presence, a trace of his glory" (*Evangelium Vitae*, 34).

Indeed, the human person has been endowed with a very exalted dignity, which is rooted in the intimate bond that unites him with his Creator: a reflection of God's own reality shines out in the human person, in every person, whatever the stage or condition of his life.

—**Pope Benedict XVI,** Address to the Pontifical Academy, February 27, 2006

Grow!

1. By their stance against Pharaoh's command, Shiphrah and Puah risked their lives to defend life. What situations or crises have you faced in which you had to take a courageous stand? What happened? How did your trust in God grow?

_____

_____

_____

_____

_____

2. When has fear prevented you from taking a stand? What were you afraid of? Where those fears reasonable? What are some ways to overcome fear in such situations?

_____

_____

_____

_____

_____

3. Shiphrah and Puah were not passive in the crisis in which they found themselves; instead, they acted decisively. How is passivity in difficult situations a temptation for you? What can lead you to act decisively?

_____

_____

_____

_____

_____

4. In our secular society, we are often called to stand up for gospel values and truth, but it's important to do so with charity. How often do you find yourself discussing controversial issues with co-workers or family or friends? What are some ways you can be loving and respectful during such discussions even when you don't agree with someone's viewpoint?

_____

_____

_____

_____

_____

5. How do you respond to immigrants and refugees? With understanding and acceptance or with fear and apprehension? In what practical ways might you reach out to welcome a newcomer in your neighborhood, at work, or in your parish?

_____

_____

_____

_____

_____

▶ In the Spotlight
Irena Sendler, Woman of Conviction and Courage

Irena Sendler was a Catholic social worker who joined the Polish underground and risked her life to rescue hundreds of Jewish children from the Warsaw ghetto during World War II. By managing to get a pass that enabled her to enter the ghetto legally, Irena was able to visit daily to establish contacts and to bring in food, medicine, and clothing.

Irena smuggled children out of the ghetto in ambulances, garbage cans, toolboxes, cartloads of goods, potato sacks, and even coffins. Sometimes she took them out through a church with two entrances, one on the ghetto side and the other opening into the Aryan side of Warsaw. With the help of workers at Warsaw's social welfare department, Irena secured hundreds of false documents with forged signatures, giving the Jewish children temporary identities.

The children were taken to private homes, orphanages, and convents. "I sent most of the children to religious establishments," Irena recalled. "I knew that I could count on the Sisters. No one ever refused to take a child from me."

The only record of the children's true identities was kept by Irena, in a coded form, in glass jars buried beneath an apple tree in her neighbor's backyard, right across the street from the German barracks. Irena hoped she would be able to locate the children after the war ended and inform them of their past. In all, the jars contained the names of 2,500 children.

On October 20, 1943, Irena was arrested and imprisoned by the Gestapo. She was severely tortured but refused to betray any of her associates, the children in hiding, or those sheltering them. Irena was sentenced to death, but while she awaited execution, a German soldier took her to an "additional interrogation." Once they were outside the prison, he shouted in Polish, "Run!" The next day Irena found her name on the list of the executed Poles. Underground members had managed to stop her execution by bribing the Germans, and Irena continued her work under a false identity.

When the war ended, Irena dug up the jars and used the coded notes to reunite the children she had placed in adoptive families with their relatives scattered across Europe. Most of the children, however, had lost their families in Nazi concentration camps. After the war, she helped establish orphanages as well as homes for the elderly.

In 1965, the Yad Vashem organization in Jerusalem awarded Irena with the title "Righteous Among the Nations," and she was made an honorary citizen of Israel. She received the Order of the White Eagle, Poland's highest civilian decoration, and in 2007, Israel and Poland supported her as a candidate for the Nobel Peace Prize.

Irena Sendler died in Warsaw in 2008 at the age of ninety-eight.

Reflect!

1. God put Shiphrah and Puah as well as the mother of Moses and Pharaoh's daughter in their particular positions in life in order to carry out his purposes for the salvation of the Israelites—and ultimately, our salvation too. Like these women, we are where we are not by accident but by God's design.

   Reflect on possible reasons why God has put you where you are right now. Consider the present season of your life; your role in your family; your financial resources; your talents, skills, and abilities; your important relationships; your sphere of influence; and your profession. Is there something in particular that God may be asking you to do in your present circumstances to further his purposes?

2. Reflect on the following Scripture passages to guide and strengthen you in keeping the commands of the Lord and living uprightly:

   > Do not enter the path of the wicked,
   >   and do not walk in the way of evildoers.
   > Avoid it; do not go on it;
   >   turn away from it and pass on. . . .
   > But the path of the righteous is like the light of dawn,
   >   which shines brighter and brighter until full day.
   > (Proverbs 4:14-15, 18)

The fear of the Lord is glory and exultation,
   and gladness and a crown of rejoicing.
The fear of the Lord delights the heart,
   and gives gladness and joy and long life.
Those who fear the Lord will have a happy end;
   on the day of their death they will be blessed.
(Sirach 1:11-13)

[Paul to Timothy:] God did not give us a spirit of cowardice, but rather a spirit of power and of love and of self-discipline. Do not be ashamed, then, of the testimony about our Lord or of me his prisoner, but join with me in suffering for the gospel, relying on the power of God, who saved us and called us with a holy calling, not according to our works but according to his own purpose and grace. (2 Timothy 1:7-9)

▶ In the Spotlight
Staying Seated to Take a Stand

On December 1, 1955, a bus driver ordered Rosa Parks to give up her seat in the "colored" section of the bus to a white passenger after the "white" section was filled. She refused. As Parks later explained, "When he saw me still sitting, he asked if I was going to stand up, and I said, 'No, I'm not.' And he said, 'Well, if you don't stand up, I'm going to have to call the police and have you arrested.' I said, 'You may do that.'"

On Sunday, December 4, plans for the Montgomery Bus Boycott were announced at black churches in the area. The following day Rosa was tried on charges of disorderly conduct and for violating a segregation ordinance of the Montgomery city code, even though she technically had not taken a "white-only" seat—she had been in the "colored" section. Rosa was found guilty in a trial that lasted thirty minutes; she was fined ten dollars, plus four dollars in court costs. She appealed her conviction and formally challenged the legality of racial segregation.

During the yearlong bus boycott, thousands of blacks walked to work rather than ride on segregated buses. The protest continued until the U.S. Supreme Court overturned the city ordinance requiring segregation on public buses. Parks' act of civil disobedience and the Montgomery Bus Boycott became iconic symbols in the civil rights movement in America and fostered efforts against racial segregation in other countries as well.

Rosa Parks suffered for the bold stance she had taken in refusing to give up her seat on the bus: she was fired from her job as a seamstress and received death threats for years afterwards. Not long after the boycott ended, she moved to Detroit, where she briefly found similar work. Later she worked for Democratic congressman John Conyers and cofounded a nonprofit institute to help youths in Detroit. She also traveled around the country to lecture on civil rights. In 1996, she was awarded the Presidential Medal of Freedom.

Parks died in October 2005 at the age of ninety-two. She was the first woman to lie in honor at the Capitol Rotunda. On December 1, 2005, the fiftieth anniversary of Parks' arrest, President George W. Bush directed that a statue of Parks be placed in the U.S. Capitol's National Statuary Hall, stating, "By placing her statue in the heart of the nation's Capitol, we commemorate her work for a more perfect union, and we commit ourselves to continue to struggle for justice for every American."

Act!

Is there an important moral or ethical issue facing you at work or in your community, or a social justice issue being considered by your state legislature or in the US Congress? If you sense God calling you to do something, ask him for the courage to be bold as well as for the grace to be kind and loving to those with whom you disagree.

Pray these Intercessory Prayers for Pro-Life Advocates prepared by the United States Catholic Conference of Bishops (USCCB):

For those who long for the equality of all persons: that their dedication to the unborn, the old, the condemned, and the forgotten may grow every day. *We pray to the Lord.*

For all who work for an end to abortion: that they might be strengthened by prayer, and that God might reward them for their goodness. *We pray to the Lord.*

For all those who work to promote the Gospel of Life: that God might reward them for their goodness. *We pray to the Lord.*

For those who work to defend the lives of the unborn, the sick, the infirm, and the aged; those who defend humanity's inalienable right to life. *We pray to the Lord.*

For all who work for an end to the culture of death, especially for our brothers and sisters from other churches, ecclesial communions, and religions, that love for the Gospel of Life might draw us closer in Christ. *We pray to the Lord.*

▶ In the Spotlight
Called to Be "Protectors"

In his inaugural homily, Pope Francis called us to be "protectors" of people and of creation.

How does Joseph respond to his calling to be the protector of Mary, Jesus, and the Church? By being constantly attentive to God, open to the signs of God's presence, and receptive to God's plans, and not simply to his own. . . . Joseph is a "protector" because he is able to hear God's voice and be guided by his will; and for this reason he is all the more sensitive to the persons entrusted to his safekeeping. He can look at things realistically, he is in touch with his surroundings, he can make truly wise decisions. In him, dear friends, we learn how to respond to God's call, readily and willingly, but we also see the core of the Christian vocation, which is Christ! Let us protect Christ in our lives, so that we can protect others, so that we can protect creation!

The vocation of being a "protector," however, is not just something involving us Christians alone; it also has a prior dimension which is simply human, involving everyone. It means protecting all creation, the beauty of the created world, as the Book of Genesis tells us and as St. Francis of Assisi showed us. It means respecting each of God's creatures and respecting the environment in which we live. It means protecting people, showing loving concern for each and every person, especially children, the elderly, those in need, who are often the last we think about. It means caring for one another in our families: husbands and wives first protect one another, and then, as parents, they care for their children, and children themselves, in time, protect their parents. It means building sincere friendships in which we protect one another in trust, respect, and goodness. In the end, everything has been entrusted to our protection, and all of us are responsible for it. Be protectors of God's gifts!

—**Pope Francis,** Inaugural Homily, March 19, 2013

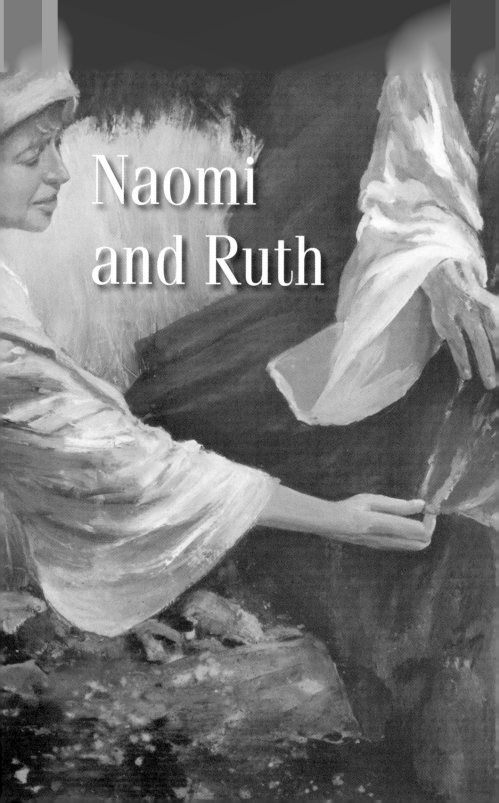

Naomi
and Ruth

Ruth 1:1-18, 22; 2:1-3, 8-12; 4:13-17

¹:¹In the days when the judges ruled, there was a famine in the land, and a certain man of Bethlehem in Judah went to live in the country of Moab,

> The book of Ruth shows how God uses human faithfulness and generosity to restore life, but it also honestly portrays the pain that great losses can inflict on us.
> —**Kevin Perrotta,** *Love Crosses Boundaries: Jonah/Ruth*

he and his wife and two sons. ²The name of the man was Elimelech and the name of his wife Naomi, and the names of his two sons were Mahlon and Chilion; they were Ephrathites from Bethlehem in Judah. They went into the country of Moab and remained there. ³But Elimelech, the husband of Naomi, died, and she was left with her two sons. ⁴These took Moabite wives; the name of the one was Orpah and the name of the other Ruth. When they had lived there about ten years, ⁵both Mahlon and Chilion also died, so that the woman was left without her two sons and her husband. ⁶Then she started to return with her daughters-in-law from the country of Moab, for she had heard in the country of Moab that the LORD had considered his people and given them food. ⁷So she set out from the place where she had been living, she and her two daughters-in-law, and they went on their way to go back to the land of Judah. ⁸But Naomi said to her two daughters-in-law, "Go back each of you to your mother's house. May the LORD deal kindly with you, as you have dealt with the dead and with me. ⁹The LORD grant that you may find security, each of you in the house of your husband." Then she kissed them, and they wept aloud. ¹⁰They said to her, "No, we will return with you to your people." ¹¹But Naomi said, "Turn back, my daughters, why will you go with me? Do I still have sons in my womb that they may become your husbands? ¹²Turn back, my daughters, go your way, for I am too old to have a husband. Even if I thought there was hope for me, even if I should have a husband tonight and bear sons, ¹³would you then wait until they were grown? Would you then refrain from marrying? No, my daughters, it has been far more bitter for me than for you, because the hand of the LORD has turned against me." ¹⁴Then they wept aloud again. Orpah kissed her mother-in-law, but Ruth clung to her. ¹⁵So she said, "See, your sister-in-law has gone back to her people and to her gods; return after your sister-in-law." ¹⁶But Ruth said, "Do not press me to leave you / or to turn back from following you! / Where you go, I will go; / where you lodge, I will lodge; / your people shall be my people, / and your God my God. / ¹⁷Where you die, I will die— / there will I be buried. / May the LORD do thus and so to me, / and more as well, / if even death parts me from you!" ¹⁸When Naomi saw that she was determined to go with her, she said no more to her. . . . ²²So Naomi returned together with Ruth the Moabite, her daughter-in-law, who came back with her from the country of Moab. They came to Bethlehem at the beginning of the barley harvest.

²:¹Now Naomi had a kinsman on her husband's side, a prominent rich man, of the family of Elimelech, whose name was Boaz. ²And Ruth the Moabite said to Naomi, "Let me go to the field and glean among the ears of grain, behind someone in whose sight I may find favor." She said to her, "Go, my daughter." ³So she went. She came and gleaned in the field behind the reapers. As it happened, she came to the part of the field belonging to Boaz, who was of the family of Elimelech. . . . ⁸Then Boaz said to Ruth, "Now listen, my daughter, do not go to glean in another field or leave this one, but keep close to my young women. ⁹Keep your eyes on the field that is being reaped, and follow behind them. I have ordered the young men not to bother you. If you get thirsty, go to the vessels and drink from what the young men have drawn." ¹⁰Then she fell prostrate, with her face to the ground, and said to him, "Why have I found favor in your sight, that you should take notice of me, when I am a foreigner?" ¹¹But Boaz answered her, "All that you have done for your mother-in-law since the death of your husband has been fully told me, and how you left your father and mother and your native land and came to a people that you did not know before. ¹²May the LORD reward you for your

deeds, and may you have a full reward from the LORD, the God of Israel, under whose wings you have come for refuge!"

⁴:¹³So Boaz took Ruth and she became his wife. When they came together, the LORD made her conceive, and she bore a son. ¹⁴Then the women said to Naomi, "Blessed be the LORD, who has not left you this day without next-of-kin; and may his name be renowned in Israel! ¹⁵He shall be to you a restorer of life and a nourisher of your old age; for your daughter-in-law who loves you, who is more to you than seven sons, has borne him." ¹⁶Then Naomi took the child and laid him in her bosom, and became his nurse. ¹⁷The women of the neighborhood gave him a name, saying, "A son has been born to Naomi." They named him Obed; he became the father of Jesse, the father of David.

> The opening of the Book of Ruth is marked with suffering, loss, grief, and emptiness, but its conclusion reflects restoration, fullness of life, and God's faithfulness.

(If possible, read the entire Book of Ruth.)

The Book of Ruth is a significant "chapter" in the centuries-long story of God's unique way of fulfilling his promise to send a Savior to his chosen people, Israel—and to all humankind. Although the book was written at a later date, its setting is "in the days when the judges ruled" (Ruth 1:1), approximately 1200–1050 BC. Joshua had led the Israelites in conquering parts of Canaan after their deliverance from Egypt. The "judges" were tribal heroes who became military leaders and magistrates after Joshua's death.

The opening of this story is marked by suffering, loss, grief, and emptiness, but its conclusion reflects restoration, fullness of life, and God's faithfulness. Thus, it is a story of what Baptist pastor and biblical scholar John Piper has called "sweet and bitter providence." Naomi's life was plagued by misfortune and tragedy. She and her husband, Elimelech, along with their sons, Mahlon and Chilion, had fled from a famine in Judah, hoping for a better life in the foreign country of Moab. But there Elimelech died; some years later Naomi lost her sons as well. Neither Orpah nor Ruth, her sons' wives, had borne children. Not only did Naomi mourn the deaths of her husband and sons, but she also suffered the loss of the support usually provided by male family members. Thus, bereaved and deprived, Naomi said in sorrow, "Call me no longer Naomi [pleasant], / call me Mara [bitter], / for the Almighty has dealt bitterly with me" (Ruth 1:20).

Ruth, herself a childless widow, chose to leave her homeland and family to accompany Naomi back to Bethlehem rather than abandon her mother-in-law and return to her parents' home for security. Her loyalty is expressed in deeply moving words: "Do not press me to leave you / or to turn back from following you! / Where you go, I will go; / where you lodge, I will lodge; / your people shall be my people, / and your God my God. / Where you die, I will die— / there will I be buried" (Ruth 1:16-17). Her decision—surely fraught with risk—was undergirded by her love and courage. In choosing to be faithful to Naomi, Ruth also then chose to take on Naomi's God, the God of Israel, and be faithful to him.

When the two widows settle in Bethlehem, they have no way of supporting themselves. So Ruth gleans the fields of Boaz, a relative of Naomi's dead husband, Elimelech (Ruth 2:1-2). According to Mosaic law, if a married man died without children, his closest male relative was required to marry his widow and raise up heirs (Deuteronomy 25:5-10; Genesis 38). Aware of this legal practice, called "levirate marriage," and hoping to use it to their advantage, Naomi astutely formed a plan to help Ruth gain Boaz's favor. (This plan unfolds in great detail in chapters 2, 3, and 4.)

Ruth readily follows her mother-in-law's shrewd guidance and prudent directions, and Boaz shows willingness and kindness in responsibly exercising his right to marry Ruth after a nearer relative declined. In keeping with the Law, Boaz says, "I acquired from the hand of Naomi all that belonged to Elimelech and all that belonged to Chilion and Mahlon. I have also acquired Ruth the Moabite, the wife of Mahlon, to be my wife, to maintain the dead man's name on his inheritance, in order that the name of the dead may not be cut off from his kindred and from the gate of his native place" (Ruth 4:9-10). As popular art historian and author Sr. Wendy Beckett notes,

> The story of Ruth, neat and compact, could be called a tender romance. However, the romance is not really between man and woman—though that is still there—but between mother and daughter-in-law. . . . The sweetness of the relationship between Ruth and Naomi is extraordinarily touching, and so is the gentlemanly conduct of Boaz. Everybody in this book acts well. This is how we want God's people to move towards their destiny, with love and dignity and consideration of others. (*Sister Wendy's Bible Treasury*)

The Book of Ruth ends with chapter 4 and is a beautiful illustration of God's faithfulness and mercy to Naomi and Ruth. The town elders witness Boaz's legal proceedings and pray, "May the LORD make the woman who is coming into your house like Rachel and Leah, who together built up the house of Israel. May you produce children in Ephrathah and bestow a name in Bethlehem" (Ruth 4:11).

"The LORD made [Ruth] conceive," and she bears a son whom she and Boaz name Obed (Ruth 4:13, 17). The birth of this child brings great joy and comfort to his grandmother, Naomi, whose friends and neighbors exclaim, "Blessed be the LORD, who has not left you this day without next-of-kin; and may his name be renowned in Israel! He shall be to you a restorer of life and a nourisher of your old age; for your daughter-in-law who loves you, who is more to you than seven sons, has borne him" (4:14-15). Obed grows up to become the father of Jesse and the grandfather of David, the most renowned king of Israel. The book closes with a genealogy (4:18-22) tracing the descendants of Boaz down to the time of King David (1004–965 BC), which seems to indicate the story was written around this time.

Ultimately, with Ruth's marriage to Boaz and the birth of Obed, great blessings come out of the losses, emptiness, and pain that both of these women have endured. Naomi delights in her grandson, and Ruth, as an ancestor of King David, gains the honor of being among the forebears of Christ the Messiah. For as Isaiah later prophesied, "A shoot shall come out from the stump of Jesse, / and a branch shall grow out of his roots" (11:1)—a foretelling of the Messiah to come from the line of Obed, Jesse, and David. And as the prophet Micah declared about Bethlehem, the hometown of Naomi, Boaz, Obed, and David, "From you shall come forth for me / one who is to rule in Israel, / whose origin is from of old, / from ancient days" (5:2).

Finally, the Evangelist Matthew names Ruth in the family record of Jesus the Messiah—the son of David, born in Bethlehem—that opens his Gospel (1:5-6). Through her, a Moabite, the universality of the messianic promise is foreshadowed.

The story of Naomi and Ruth gives us hope and assurance that the Lord is able—and eager!—to bring redemption, restoration, and blessing out of our own pain and loss, no matter how trying our circumstances may be. In the crisis that Ruth faced, she could have chosen the easier path by returning to her homeland, a place of security. Instead, she took the riskier decision to accompany Naomi to Bethlehem because she did not want to leave Naomi alone. The Lord rewarded her faithfulness by redeeming the tragic situation that both women faced. And not only were Ruth and Naomi blessed; because Ruth became the forebear of King David and ultimately Jesus, we have become recipients of that blessing.

Understand!

1. At the opening of this story, how did Naomi's losses affect her? What did she encourage Orpah and Ruth to do? What reasons for this did Naomi give both of her daughters-in-law?

_____

_____

_____

_____

_____

2. Why, in your opinion, did Ruth choose to accompany Naomi to Bethlehem? What verses in the scriptural text support your answer? What sacrifices did Ruth's decision entail and cost her? What challenges do you think she faced as a foreigner in Bethlehem?

_____

_____

_____

_____

_____

3. What qualities of Ruth are most striking to you? Of Naomi? Which strengths did each of these women show? Do any of Naomi's or Ruth's actions disturb you? If so, why?

_____

_____

_____

_____

_____

4. Give several examples of "sweetness" that you see as the Book of Ruth unfolds. What has this story of Naomi and Ruth taught you about God? About how to face the vicissitudes of life?

_____

_____

_____

_____

_____

5. Why do you think God chose to include Ruth, a Moabite, in Jesus' family tree? Why is the Book of Ruth an important "chapter" in salvation history? Why is the fulfillment of Old Testament prophecies significant for us today?

_____

_____

_____

_____

_____

What's in a Name?

Names are quite significant in the Book of Ruth because they have very symbolic meanings. In Hebrew, "Elimelech," the name of Naomi's husband, carries several meanings: "May kingship come my way" or "God is my king." Both renderings are apt because Elimelech was of the tribe of Judah, from which King David and the Messiah were descended.

The name "Naomi" comes from *na'im* (pleasant; amiable; lively; delightful). But upon her return to Bethlehem after the death of her husband and sons, Naomi asked that her name be changed to "Mara," which means "bitter," because of the losses and sufferings that she had endured (Ruth 1:20).

The most obvious symbolic names are those of Elimelech and Naomi's two sons: "Mahlon" means "weakness" or "sickness," while "Chilion" means "perishing" or "decimated"; it can also be interpreted as "sickly," "pining," or "puny." This change may have been done on purpose by the author because the symbolic names strengthened the impact of the story.

The names of Naomi's daughters-in-law are also significant. "Orpah" is derived from *oref* (the back of the head); *le-hafnot oref* is "to turn away." Orpah turned away from Naomi and the Israelite people and went back to Moab. "Ruth" is derived from a word that can mean "satisfaction, satiety." Another form of the word refers to giving drink or refreshment, and is used in Psalm 23 to speak of a cup that "overflows" (23:5). As Scripture commentator Kevin Perrotta notes, "Ruth's name is certainly appropriate for her in terms of her character. She turns out to be a source of satisfaction and refreshment for Naomi and for many others, including ourselves" (*Prayer, Fasting, and Almsgiving: Spiritual Practices That Draw Us Closer to God*). "Ruth" is also related to a word that means "beloved," "companion," or "friend"—all of which Ruth proved to be to her mother-in-law, Naomi.

Ruth married a man called "Boaz," a name indicating "in the strength of the Lord." Together they had a son, "Obed," whose name means "workman" or "servant," pointing to his role as a servant of the Lord by becoming the father of Jesse. The name "Jesse" holds quite a wide range of meanings: "the Lord is," "the one who is," or "Yahweh is/Yahweh exists." It is possible that "Jesse" also means "gift" or "oblation." Finally, it is most likely that "David," the name of Jesse's youngest son, means "commander" or "hero"—again, a fitting attribute for the man who became the greatest of Israel's kings and forerunner of the Messiah.

Grow!

1. Recall a time when you experienced a major change in your life (for example, moving away from your familiar neighborhood, choosing a new career direction, losing a spouse). How challenging was it for you? How did you cope? How well do you feel that you adjusted to your new situation?

_____

_____

_____

_____

_____

2. Ruth was motivated by love and loyalty to accompany and support Naomi. Have you ever acted like Ruth and done something out of great love and/or commitment to another person, undeterred by what this may have cost you? Did you find joy in carrying out your decision or see fruit from it?

_____

_____

_____

_____

_____

3. What is your usual response to hardship? Bitterness and anger or trust in God? Fear and anxiety or courage and confidence? When have you seen a personal loss or adversity eventually turn out to hold some blessings for you? Explain.

_____

_____

_____

_____

_____

4. Think of someone you know whose character reminds you of Ruth. Do you know anyone like Naomi? What impact have these people had on your own life?

_____

_____

_____

_____

_____

5. What is your attitude toward those who are poverty-stricken or cannot support themselves? How can you offer help to the needy in your local community?

_____

_____

_____

_____

_____

▶ In the Spotlight
A Heart for Helping Others

One of the truths about God that we learn in Scripture is that he is eager to protect the stranger, the orphan, and the widow. He favors those in distress. But how does he do this? He doesn't just reach down from heaven and pluck them out of their problems. He uses people, often people who are struggling themselves or who have experienced past trials, to accomplish his will. For who better to help someone in need than someone who knows what it's like to be alone or downtrodden?

We see this principle at work in the lives of Ruth and Naomi. Naomi is a childless widow, crushed in spirit. She even changes her name to "Mara," which means "bitter" (Ruth 1:20). Her daughter-in-law Ruth has also been widowed and has no children of her own. But Ruth's heart goes out to Naomi, and so rather than return to her father's house, she opts to accompany Naomi when she decides to return to Israel. In the process of rescuing Naomi, Ruth ends up marrying Boaz, a wealthy and upright landowner. Not only is Naomi rescued, but so is Ruth—and she is brought closer to God!

The story of Ruth tells us that we don't have to be perfect ourselves before we can minister God's love. We simply have to be willing to offer ourselves as best we can. We may feel inadequate because we are facing our own challenges, but that may be just as God wants it. After all, the very word "compassion" means "to suffer with."

When we give ourselves to help another person, something wonderful happens. By picking up that person's cross, we meet Jesus in a powerful way—just as Simon of Cyrene did on the way to Calvary. Those who serve from the heart experience a reward in the service itself. Not only is Ruth a proof of that, but she foreshadows Jesus, whose whole life was one of service. Just as he was raised up to the Father's right hand because he emptied himself, we can be too.

—*The Word Among Us,* Daily Meditation, August 21, 2015

Reflect!

1. Reflect on a hardship or loss that you are currently dealing with. Perhaps you are adjusting to widowhood or struggling to accept the death of a son or daughter. Maybe you are caring for an elderly parent or a disabled child. Or it might be that you are facing a financial setback or you fear losing your job.

   Now give your particular care and concern to the Lord. Talk to him honestly about how you feel about your situation. Pray for guidance, wisdom, and grace for coping with the challenges—and be sure to ask the Lord to give you expectant faith to recognize that some "sweetness" and good will come out of this "bitter" difficulty.

2. Reflect on the following Scripture passages to give you perspective on the gains that can come out of suffering and pain:

   > This I call to mind,
   >   and therefore I have hope:

The steadfast love of the LORD never ceases,
    his mercies never come to an end;
they are new every morning;
    great is your faithfulness. . . .
For the Lord will not
    reject forever.
Although he causes grief, he will have compassion
    according to the abundance of his steadfast love;
for he does not willingly afflict
    or grieve anyone. (Lamentations 3:21-23; 31-33)

I consider that the sufferings of this present time are not worth comparing with the glory about to be revealed to us. For the creation waits with eager longing for the revealing of the children of God; for the creation was subjected to futility, not of its own will but by the will of the one who subjected it, in hope that the creation itself will be set free from its bondage to decay and will obtain the freedom of the glory of the children of God. (Romans 8:18-21)

We do not lose heart. Even though our outer nature is wasting away, our inner nature is being renewed day by day. For this slight momentary affliction is preparing us for an eternal weight of glory beyond all measure, because we look not at what can be seen but at what cannot be seen; for what can be seen is temporary, but what cannot be seen is eternal. (2 Corinthians 4:16-18)

▶ In the Spotlight
The Tree of Jesse

Commonly seen in Christian art, the Tree of Jesse is a visual depiction of the ancestors of Christ—a schematic family tree that presents Jesus' genealogy. Traditional pictorial representations of the Tree of Jesse show a symbolic tree or vine with spreading branches growing up out of a recumbent Jesse, the father of King David, to represent Jesus' genealogy in accordance with Isaiah's prophecy: "A shoot shall come out from the stump of Jesse, / and a branch shall grow out of his roots" (11:1). On the branches of the tree, usually surrounded by tendrils of foliage, are portrayed various figures from the lineage of Jesus, drawn from among the names listed in the Gospels of Matthew and Luke. Matthew's genealogy traces Jesus' lineage in descending order—from Abraham through Boaz (and Ruth), Obed, Jesse, and David, all the way to Joseph, the husband of Mary (1:1-17). Luke recounts the genealogy in ascending order, from Jesus back to David and then to Adam (3:23-38). Both of these genealogies permit the interpretation that Jesus is the "shoot" or "stem" of Jesse by his descent from Jesse's son, David. Mary, the mother of Jesus, is often seen in the crown of the tree, holding in her arms the child who is the fulfillment of Isaiah's prophecy.

The Tree of Jesse was often depicted in illuminated manuscripts and psalters of the medieval period. It also appears in stained glass windows, stone carvings around the portals of medieval cathedrals, frescoes and wall paintings, tapestries, and carved ivories. Many depictions of the Jesse Tree were popular in the Gothic Revival art of the nineteenth century; the twentieth century also produced numerous fine examples.

In recent years, many Christians have begun to use a derivative of the Jesse Tree during Advent, decorating a tree branch, poster, calendar, or banner over the course of the season with symbols that represent figures from Jesus' genealogy. For example, Ruth is represented by a sheaf of wheat because she gleaned in Boaz's fields, while a harp is the emblem for David, who wrote and sang many of the psalms. Symbols from other Bible stories that lead up to the birth of Christ, such as a rainbow over Noah's ark and the burning bush from Exodus, are also often included to help children understand the history of our salvation.

Act!

Follow this suggestion from Catholic author Anne Costa:

Draw a timeline of your life from your birth to the present, and highlight your major losses. This could include people who have died, as well as other major losses in your life. Reflect on how you grieved and honored those losses in your life. Did you take the time to grieve? How have these losses affected your life? How have they become a part of your life?

Keeping with the image of your life as a tapestry and the dark threads as your losses, what beauty and light have come into your life to contrast the "dark threads" of sorrow and loss? What gifts have you been given along your road to healing? (*Lord, I Hurt! The Grace of Forgiveness and the Road to Healing*)

▶ In the Spotlight
The Loyalty of Love

Ruth showed great faithfulness to Naomi, standing by her in a time of grief and sorrow and trusting in her God. Here is the story of another faithful daughter staying at her mother's side as she was dying, written by Dorothy Day, convert, social activist, journalist, and cofounder of the Catholic Worker Movement:

It made me happy that I could be with my mother the last few weeks of her life, and for the last ten days at her bedside daily and hourly. Sometimes I thought to myself that it was like being present at a birth to sit by a dying person and see their intentness on what is happening to them. It almost seems that one is absorbed in a struggle, a fearful, grim, physical struggle, to breathe, to swallow, to live. And so, I kept thinking to myself, how necessary it is for one of their loved ones to be beside them, to pray for them, to offer up prayers for them unceasingly, as well as to do all those little offices one can. When my daughter was a little tiny girl, she said to me once, "When I get to be a great big woman and you are a little tiny girl, I'll take care of you," and I thought of that when I had to feed my mother by the spoonful and urge her to eat her custard. How good God was to me, to let me be there. I had prayed so constantly that I would be beside her when she died; for years I had offered up that prayer. And God granted it quite literally. I was there, holding her hand, and she just turned her head and sighed. That was her last breath, that little sigh; and her hand was warm in mine for a long time after.

—**Dorothy Day,** "Notes by the Way"

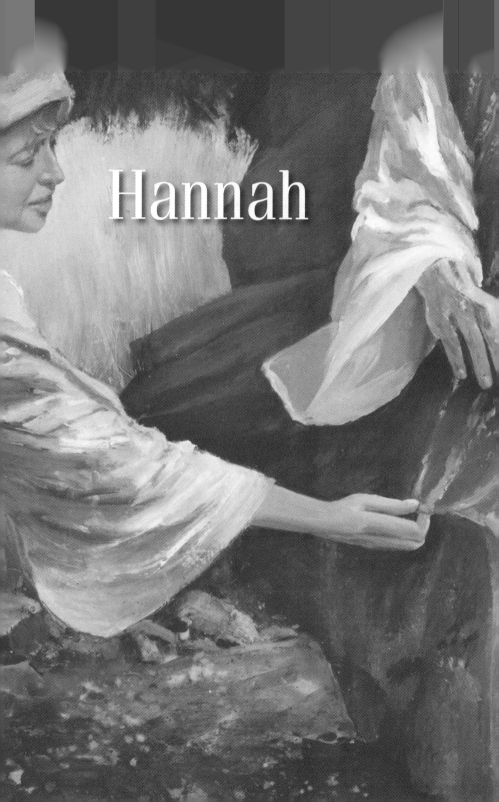

Hannah

1 Samuel 1:1-28; 2:18-21

1:1There was a certain man of Ramathaim, a Zuphite from the hill country of Ephraim, whose name was Elkanah son of Jeroham son of Elihu son of Tohu son of Zuph, an Ephraimite. 2He had two wives; the name of the one was Hannah, and the name of the other Peninnah. Peninnah had children, but Hannah had no children.

3Now this man used to go up year by year from his town to worship and to sacrifice to the LORD of hosts at Shiloh, where the two sons of Eli, Hophni and Phinehas, were priests of the LORD. 4On the day when Elkanah sacrificed, he would give portions to his wife Peninnah and to all her sons and daughters; 5but to Hannah he gave a double portion, because he loved her, though the LORD had closed her womb. 6Her rival used to provoke her severely, to irritate her, because the LORD had closed her womb. 7So it went on year by year; as often as she went up to the house of the LORD, she used to provoke her. Therefore Hannah wept and would not eat. 8Her husband Elkanah said to her, "Hannah, why do you weep? Why do you not eat? Why is your heart sad? Am I not more to you than ten sons?"

> Hannah stood expectantly before the Lord when she had nothing to give but her anguish. And God, who is rich in mercy, did not disappoint her.
> — Craig Morrison, O Carm, *The Word Among Us*

9After they had eaten and drunk at Shiloh, Hannah rose and presented herself before the LORD. Now Eli the priest was sitting on the seat beside the doorpost of the temple of the LORD. 10She was deeply distressed and prayed to the LORD, and wept bitterly. 11She made this vow: "O LORD of hosts, if only you will look on the misery of your servant, and remember me, and not forget your servant, but will give to your servant a male child, then I will set him before you as a nazirite until the day of his death. He shall drink neither wine nor intoxicants, and no razor shall touch his head."

¹²As she continued praying before the LORD, Eli observed her mouth. ¹³Hannah was praying silently; only her lips moved, but her voice was not heard; therefore Eli thought she was drunk. ¹⁴So Eli said to her, "How long will you make a drunken spectacle of yourself? Put away your wine." ¹⁵But Hannah answered, "No, my lord, I am a woman deeply troubled; I have drunk neither wine nor strong drink, but I have been pouring out my soul before the LORD. ¹⁶Do not regard your servant as a worthless woman, for I have been speaking out of my great anxiety and vexation all this time." ¹⁷Then Eli answered, "Go in peace; the God of Israel grant the petition you have made to him." ¹⁸And she said, "Let your servant find favor in your sight." Then the woman went to her quarters, ate and drank with her husband, and her countenance was sad no longer.

¹⁹They rose early in the morning and worshiped before the LORD; then they went back to their house at Ramah. Elkanah knew his wife Hannah, and the LORD remembered her. ²⁰In due time Hannah conceived and bore a son. She named him Samuel, for she said, "I have asked him of the LORD."

²¹The man Elkanah and all his household went up to offer to the LORD the yearly sacrifice, and to pay his vow. ²²But Hannah did not go up, for she said to her husband, "As soon as the child is weaned, I will bring him, that he may appear in the presence of the LORD, and remain there forever; I will offer him as a nazirite for all time." ²³Her husband Elkanah said to her, "Do what seems best to you, wait until you have weaned him; only—may the LORD establish his word." So the woman remained and nursed her son, until she weaned him. ²⁴When she had weaned him, she took him up with her, along with a three-year-old bull, an ephah of flour, and a skin of wine. She brought him to the house of the LORD at Shiloh; and the child was young. ²⁵Then they slaughtered the bull, and they brought the child to Eli. ²⁶And she said, "Oh, my lord! As you live, my lord, I am the woman who was standing here in your presence, praying to the LORD. ²⁷For this child I prayed; and the LORD has granted me the petition that I made to him. ²⁸Therefore

I have lent him to the LORD; as long as he lives, he is given to the LORD."

She left him there for the LORD.

²:¹⁸Samuel was ministering before the LORD, a boy wearing a linen ephod. ¹⁹His mother used to make for him a little robe and take it to him each year, when she went up with her husband to offer the yearly sacrifice. ²⁰Then Eli would bless Elkanah and his wife, and say, "May the LORD repay you with children by this woman for the gift that she made to the LORD"; and then they would return to their home.

²¹And the LORD took note of Hannah; she conceived and bore three sons and two daughters. And the boy Samuel grew up in the presence of the LORD.

(See also 1 Samuel 2:1-11.)

Hannah was burdened with grief and sorrow: she longed to be a mother yet was childless (1 Samuel 1:2). Her infertility was a source of anguish and misery. Deeply distressed, Hannah was so spent with crying that she couldn't even eat (1:7).

In a society in which infertility was a public disgrace, the failure to bear children was an especially terrible burden. No only did Hannah experience personal grief and heartache, but she also endured shame and the ridicule of Peninnah, Elkanah's other wife. (Having two wives was a practice common and acceptable in the culture of that time.) Peninnah had borne many children and never let Hannah forget her childlessness, taunting and provoking her (1 Samuel 1:6). Yet Elkanah loved Hannah and treated her with compassion and tenderness (1:5, 8). Surely he would have wanted Hannah to bear a child, but he did not reject or upbraid her for not becoming pregnant. As Carmelite Scripture scholar Craig Morrison noted, "[Elkanah's] reaction to her infertility is not typical for men of that culture. When Sarah was unable to conceive, for example, Abraham complained to God that he wanted an heir (Genesis 15). Clearly, Elkanah and Hannah have a unique relationship. Theirs is a love story. Still, Hannah wants to be a mother and cannot be consoled."

Each year the whole family went to the shrine at Shiloh to offer sacrifice to the Lord (there was as yet no temple in Jerusalem). It was especially at those times, when Elkanah would give a "double portion" of the meat from the animal sacrifice to Hannah because of his love for her, that Peninnah—probably out of jealousy—would provoke her. Yet Hannah had not given up hope: this particular year, as she prayed to the Lord in her distress, she was also filled with determination. Weeping bitterly, she asked the Lord to look on her misery and to "remember" her. It was a request insisting that God listen, a prayer reflecting great faith. Then Hannah made an amazing promise: if the Lord would grant her a son, she would, in gratitude, dedicate the child to the Lord from birth and give him to God's service (1 Samuel 1:11).

When Eli, the priest serving at Shiloh, saw how Hannah prayed, silently yet with her lips moving, he thought she was drunk. However, Hannah explained, "I have been pouring out my soul before the LORD" (1 Samuel 1:15). This image reminds us of Job, another biblical character who endured intense suffering and likened his anguish to his soul being "poured out within me" (Job 30:16).

Once Eli realized that Hannah was not "a worthless woman" but rather one earnestly speaking to the Lord of her troubles, he said, "Go in peace; the God of Israel grant the petition you have made to him" (1 Samuel 1:16, 17). Then we read in verse 18, "The woman went to her quarters, ate and drank with her husband, and her countenance was sad no longer." Author Heidi Bratton points out just how striking this scene is: "Even more amazing than what Eli said is what Hannah did. She changed her attitude and embraced the peace that Eli had offered her." Bratton continues,

Hannah's encounter with God in the temple marks the height of conflict in her life story. To the temple she brings her greatest burden, childlessness, and basically throws it at God's feet. Then without any tangible proof that God will positively answer her prayer, she walks out, leaving her burden behind. Hannah's peace is restored, not because God has yet answered her prayer, but because, with the help of Eli, she has handed her burden to God and trusted him with it.

This is good news for those of us who are carrying great burdens! If we are as authentic with God as Hannah was in presenting our burdens to him and then leave them with God in faith and trust, we also can have the peace that Hannah experienced. *(Finding God's Peace in Everyday Challenges)*

Hannah's determined faith in God and the offering of her child to God's service would greatly impact the course of Israel's history—and our own salvation history as well.

Although Eli didn't know specifically what Hannah was praying for, his response to her—"the God of Israel grant the petition you have made to him" (1 Samuel 1:17)—prophetically anticipated the meaning of the name of the son she would later bear. "Samuel," as Hannah called her child, means in Hebrew "asked of God," "heard by God," or "name of God" (1:20).

After worshipping before the Lord, Hannah and Elkanah returned home to Ramah. Then, "Elkanah knew his wife Hannah, and the LORD remembered her. In due time Hannah conceived and bore a son" (1 Samuel 1:19-20). After Samuel was weaned, Hannah fulfilled her promise to the Lord by bringing the three-year-old child to live with the priest, Eli, at the shrine of the LORD in Shiloh: "For this child I prayed; and the LORD has granted me the petition that I made to him. Therefore I have lent him to the Lord; as long as he lives, he is given to the LORD" (1:27-28). Hannah didn't, as we might expect, grieve that she would see her child only once a year (2:19); rather, she proclaimed her joy and faith in God's goodness in a canticle of praise (2:1-10). And in the years to come, as Samuel "grew up in the presence of the LORD," God graciously blessed Hannah and Elkanah with three more sons and two daughters (2:21). We hear echoes of the Lord's graciousness in Psalm 113:9: "He gives the barren woman a home, / making her the joyous mother of children."

Hannah's determined faith in God and the offering of her child to God's service would greatly impact the course of Israel's history—and our own salvation history as well. Samuel would grow up to be one of Israel's greatest judges; it was he who would carry out God's purposes for his chosen people by anointing Israel's first king, Saul, and its greatest king, David. And it would be into the house of David that Jesus, the promised Messiah and Savior of the world, would be born.

Hannah found herself in a crisis that seemed to have no end. Yet instead of keeping a stiff upper lip and bearing this cross, she flung herself before the Lord and poured out her anguish to him. Hannah was not afraid to "get real" with God. She was completely honest, letting him know how deeply painful her situation was. Her honesty before the Lord gives each of us the courage and determination to bring our own heartaches, unfulfilled hopes, and disappointed dreams before the Lord. May we have the grace, like Hannah, to hand over our burdens to God and to trust in him, even when we don't know how God will answer our prayers.

Understand!

1. Note the adjectives and verbs used in 1 Samuel 1:1-18 to describe how Hannah felt about herself and her barrenness. How did Hannah respond to her infertility? What did she do about her deep disappointment and her strong desire to have a child?

_____

_____

_____

_____

_____

2. What impression do you gain of Elkanah from 1 Samuel 1:3-5, 8, and 21-23? From 1 Samuel 2:19-20? How did Elkanah respond to Hannah? What does this show about his character? In what particular ways was Elkanah loving and supportive of Hannah?

_____

_____

_____

_____

_____

3. Reflect on the progression of events in Hannah's life and pinpoint her various postures throughout the course of these events. How would you describe Hannah's disposition toward Elkanah? Toward the Lord? Toward Eli and his words to her?

_____

_____

_____

_____

_____

4. How did Hannah come before the Lord to make her request to him for a child? What characterized her prayer? What did Hannah promise to the Lord if he would give her a male child?

_____

_____

_____

_____

_____

5. What have you learned about Hannah from her prayers? From her actions?

_____

_____

_____

_____

_____

▶ In the Spotlight
Called to Be a Life Bearer

I love being a woman, and I especially love being a Catholic woman because it is through my faith that I have come to truly appreciate the deep mystery and joy of my feminine nature. I have come to understand that I am called to be a life bearer who possesses a warrior spirit and a servant's heart. With Mary as my model, I pray to be clothed in gentleness and propelled by love. I strive to embody a quiet spirit that is nevertheless strong and resolute. Essentially, I seek to be an authentic woman after God's own heart.

For me, the greatest joy about being a woman comes from being a mother, but for many years I didn't know if I'd ever be able to have a child. When the doctor told me that I couldn't get pregnant, it was a difficult reality to embrace. I prayed and prayed for a miracle, all the while believing that it was possible. After seven long years, God did answer my prayer with a daughter who is now eighteen years old.

But during those years when I was yearning for motherhood, God showed me how I was blessed to offer my maternal gifts in a spiritual way to others. Every woman has these gifts because God has written them on her heart, and they are present and available even when physical motherhood is not possible. A life bearer is someone who affirms, encourages, and helps others to live more deeply and joyfully. In a special way, women are equipped to enkindle life and inspire others to reach their fullest potential. Spiritual motherhood is a genuine opportunity for women to share their gifts with others in a powerful and much-needed way in our world today.

Authentic women are born, not made. They are living out their deepest truth: that they are created in the image and likeness of God and that they are fearfully and wonderfully made. That is the reality that brings us joy. It's time to recover that truth for our sake and for the sake of generations to come.
—**Anne Costa,** *Breaking into Joy: Meditations for Living in the Love of Christ*

Grow!

1. When have you asked the Lord to "look at your misery" and "remember" you? (cf. 1 Samuel 1:11). What did God do in answer to your prayer? How have you experienced the Lord's compassion, even if your prayers were not answered in the way you wanted?

_____

_____

_____

_____

_____

2. Peninnah mocked and provoked Hannah, but Elkanah showed Hannah love and compassion. Have you ever suffered rejection or been ridiculed because of your hopes and dreams? Who in your life right now best understands your needs and desires and is supportive of you?

_____

_____

_____

_____

_____

3. Imagine Hannah's thoughts and emotions when she gave birth to Samuel—and then "gave" him to the Lord. Recall a time when you knew deep joy because of God's graciousness to you. What did you do to express your gratitude to God for his kindness and mercy to you? Have you ever offered something precious to the Lord? What did this sacrifice cost you?

_____

_____

_____

_____

_____

4. If you are a parent, what are you doing to bring your children up in the Lord and to help them know and follow the Lord's ways? How do you feel as your children make decisions that shape the course and purpose of their lives? In what ways might Hannah's

example help you as a parent to "let go" of your children and entrust them to the Lord?

_____

_____

_____

_____

_____

5. What have you learned from Hannah about "getting real" with God and expressing your true feelings to him? About faith and trusting in God? What qualities of Hannah would you most like to imitate? Why?

_____

_____

_____

_____

_____

▶ In the Spotlight
Is It Time to Let Go?

To whom do children ultimately belong? We think and speak of them as ours, but we know that people are not possessions. Though we view biblical women as daughters, sisters, wives, and mothers, we know that somewhere in the midst of that web of relatedness a person exists, solitary and simply herself. Not all cultures honor that personhood, but it is a fact of our humanity as abrupt as the cutting of the umbilical cord that began our independent lives. Family relationships, however dear and precious, are finally only roles in which we are called to participate. Jesus would teach this difficult reality with the hard words, "Who does not hate father and mother, wife and children, brothers and sisters, yes, even life itself, cannot be my disciple." He pointed to a deeper kind of kinship when he turned from his family outside the door and said, "My mother and my brother are those who hear the word of God and do it" (see Luke 14:26; 8:19-21). It's no surprise that these are among Jesus' most unpopular sayings.

It is hard to surrender belonging, harder to let go of those who are as close to us as our own breath. How did Hannah, who wept and prayed for and dreamed of a child, ever hand that baby off to the priest of Shiloh? One thing seemed clear to her: Children are finally the property of their Maker, and so she pledged her child yet unconceived to the service of God. Wise parents still make this dedication, early and often, and teach it to their children by their own example.
—Alice Camille, *God's Word Today*

Reflect!

1. This story of Hannah gives us courage to bring our anguish and sorrows to the Lord. Reflect on how you handle the disappointment of unfulfilled expectations and longings.

   At this stage of your life, what is your deepest longing and as yet unmet desire? What is your prayer or conversation with the Lord like regarding this desire? Complaining? Bold? Faith-filled? Self-pitying? Take heart, and trust in the Lord who loves, us, hears our cries, and "remembers" us.

2. Reflect on these additional instances of how God favored barren women with children: Sarah, with the birth of Isaac (Genesis 17:15-21; 18:1-15; 21:1-7); Manoah's wife, with the birth of Samson (Judges 13:2-3; 24); Elizabeth, with the birth of John the Baptist (Luke 1:5-25; 2:57). Do you identify with these women in any way?

▶ In the Spotlight
The Power of Prayer

In this story Hannah begins the tradition of private prayer. Hers is the first story of someone coming to a shrine, not for public worship or sacrifice, but simply to speak to God from the heart. She knows how to pour out her troubles to God and to remain in God's presence. She is not afraid to explain to the official religious representative [Eli] what she is doing. He is persuaded by her words and his scolding ends in a blessing. When she leaves the sanctuary Hannah's prayer is already answered; God has given peace to her heart.

—Irene Nowell, *Women in the Old Testament*

Hannah is indeed the great example and teacher of prayer. Her prayer is the word of her heart (1 Samuel 1:13). It is poured forth from the innermost center of her personality, which has been torn open by her bitterness of soul (1:10). Nevertheless her prayer is not a mere drifting of the heart on waves of emotion. Her lips move (1:13), which means that her prayer consists of definite, formulated thoughts. Deeply significant is the way she addresses God: "O Lord of hosts" (1:11). This is the first time in the Scriptures that a prayer is directed to God under this name. It signifies God as the lord and master, the leader and commander of the universe. . . . Hannah's petition ends in a vow through which she solemnly binds herself never to forget that the child is the fruit of her prayers. Although it has risen "out of the abundance of complaint and grief" (1:16), her prayer brings her already the assurance of God's mercy. "So the woman went her way and ate and her countenance was no longer sad" (1:18).

—Damasus Winzen, *Pathways in Scripture*

Act!

Hannah's prayer in 1 Samuel 2:1-10 anticipates Mary's well-known Magnificat in the New Testament (Luke 1:46-55). Hannah acknowledged and "magnified" the Lord, who looked upon her lowliness and blessed her far beyond what she had expected or anticipated. As Scripture commentator Jean-Pierre Prévost notes, "While [Hannah] celebrates her own happy reversal of fortune as a new mother (1 Samuel 2:5), she testifies to a God who exalts the feeble, the hungry, the barren, the poor and the needy, and who brings low the mighty, the satisfied, those with many children, the rich" (*God's Word Today*). Mary echoes these same sentiments centuries later in her own prayer of wonderment, praise, and gratitude to the Lord.

Recall a situation or instance in which you were deeply distressed and you experienced God at work to "raise you up from the dust" (1 Samuel 2:8) and bless you. Now, using either Hannah's canticle or Mary's Magnificat as a model, write your own prayer of praise and thanks to God for his blessings and graciousness to you.

▶ In the Spotlight
The Gift of New Life

Eduardo and his wife, Tanya, had been trying for months to conceive a child. Married in their thirties, they knew their biological clocks were ticking. Eduardo's first wife had died of cancer, leaving him with two young daughters. The older daughter, Ana, had been diagnosed with cancer when she was only ten months old and was still fighting the disease. And the younger daughter? At the age of nine, Maria had been killed when an eighteen-wheeler crushed Eduardo's BMW like tinfoil. The crash also killed Eduardo's friend, my niece Regina, whom he was thinking of marrying. Emerging from the trashed BMW with a broken arm and a heart more crushed than the car, Eduardo struggled for months to cope with this series of unexplainable tragedies. Death, it seemed, was hounding him at every turn.

But with Tanya a new life began, and they ardently hoped that soon they would hold a baby in their arms. Yet the months dragged on with no sign of new life. Finally they came to me asking that I pray over them for the gift of fertility. That I did, invoking Mary and her cousin, Elizabeth, both of whom conceived when nature said they couldn't. I also invoked the Holy Spirit, who had worked the miracle of Mary's conception of Jesus. As we prayed, Tanya had a vision of Mary and Elizabeth that consoled her; yet at the same time, she was troubled by the vision because she felt overwhelmed by her own unworthiness in the presence of these holy women. "How could someone like me win God's approval enough to be heard?" Tanya thought. Gradually the Lord healed Tanya of this self-rejection, and then she heard the doctor say, "Tanya, you're pregnant!" She gave birth to a whopping baby boy, who at eight-and-a-half pounds had to be delivered by Caesarean section.

I don't know what kind of switchboard communication went on in heaven as a result of our prayer, but certainly God gave the answer—with the bonus of a spiritual healing in the process of blessing new life in Tanya's womb.

—George T. Montague, SM, *Mary's Life in the Spirit: Meditations on a Holy Duet*

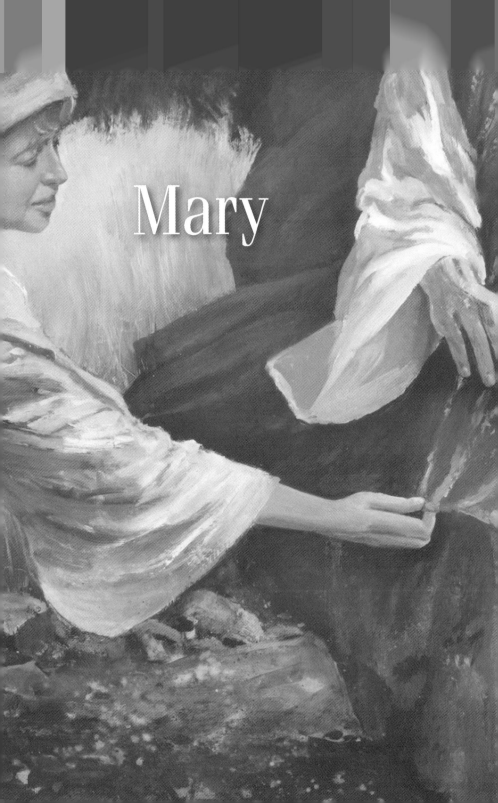

Mary

Luke 1:26-38

1:26In the sixth month the angel Gabriel was sent by God to a town in Galilee called Nazareth, 27to a virgin engaged to a man whose name was Joseph, of the house of David. The virgin's name was Mary. 28And he came to her and said, "Greetings, favored one! The Lord is with you!" 29But she was much perplexed by his words and pondered what sort of greeting this might be. 30The angel said to her, "Do not be afraid, Mary, for you have found favor with God. 31And now, you will conceive in your womb and bear a son, and you will name him Jesus. 32He will be great, and will be called the Son of the Most High, and the Lord God will give to him the throne of his ancestor David. 33He will reign over the house of Jacob forever, and of his kingdom there will be no end." 34Mary said to the angel, "How can this be, since I am a virgin?" 35The angel said to her, "The Holy Spirit will come upon you, and the power of the Most High will overshadow you; therefore the child to be born will be holy; he will be called Son of God. 36And now, your relative Elizabeth in her old age has also conceived a son; and this is the sixth month for her who was said to be barren. 37For nothing will be impossible with God." 38Then Mary said, "Here am I, the servant of the Lord; let it be with me according to your word." Then the angel departed from her.

> Mary's divine maternity, freely chosen and effected by her faith, is not merely a biological occurrence but an opening for the world to receive God's saving grace.
> —**Judith Dupré**, *Full of Grace: Encountering Mary in Faith, Art, and Life*

Matthew 1:18-25

1:18Now the birth of Jesus the Messiah took place in this way. When his mother Mary had been engaged to Joseph, but before they lived together, she was found to be with child from the Holy Spirit. [19]Her husband Joseph, being a righteous man and unwilling to expose her to public disgrace, planned to dismiss her quietly. [20]But just when he had resolved to do this, an angel of the Lord appeared to him in a dream and said, "Joseph, son of David, do not be afraid to take Mary as your wife, for the child conceived in her is from the Holy Spirit. [21]She will bear a son, and you are to name him Jesus, for he will save his people from their sins." [22]All this took place to fulfill what had been spoken by the Lord through the prophet:

[23] "Look, the virgin shall conceive and bear a son,
    and they shall name him Emmanuel,"

which means, "God is with us." [24]When Joseph awoke from sleep, he did as the angel of the Lord commanded him; he took her as his wife, [25]but had no marital relations with her until she had borne a son; and he named him Jesus.

Oh, what will Joseph—and my parents!—think of me? How will I ever explain to them everything that the angel told me and how I felt when the Holy Spirit came upon me? Of course I'm glad I said yes—I just couldn't have said no to God!—and I know that a very special child is growing inside of me. But what will happen to me now?"

Mary, probably still a young teenager, must have been overwhelmed after Gabriel left her. She must have trembled as she realized that her life had just been turned upside down by this encounter with God's messenger. What would it mean for her life that she was to bear a child who would be called the "Son of the Most High" (Luke 1:32)? Talk about an unexpected pregnancy!

Mary's first words to the angel, "How can this be, since I am a virgin?" (Luke 1:34), could sound like a skeptical demand for proof. They were, rather, an inquiry that expressed her willingness to grasp something holy and mysterious, and indicated that she wanted instructions about how this mystery was to take place. Her query reflected not doubt or disbelief but an attitude of faith that sought understanding so that she could be fully responsive and cooperative. In answer, Gabriel didn't give Mary a precise physiological explanation because Jesus' conception would transcend natural biological means. Instead, he assured her, "Nothing will be impossible for God" (1:37). The Holy Spirit would "overshadow" and empower her (1:35).

A daughter of Israel, Mary must have eagerly longed, like her fellow Jews, to see the prophetic promises that God had made to his people fulfilled. Thus, her *fiat*—"Let it be with me according to your word" (Luke 1:38)—rose out of her reverence for God's word and promises and her faith in him. Although Mary was perplexed and could not fathom all the implications of the angel's message, she had a sure, unerring conviction that God, in his goodness and wisdom, would meet her consent with grace and whatever help that she might need to carry out his will. "Mary does not know by what road she must venture, what pains she must suffer, what risks she must face," noted Pope Francis. "But she is aware that it is the Lord asking, and she entrusts herself totally to him; she abandons herself to his love. This is the faith of Mary!" (Angelus Address, December 21, 2014).

> Mary had a sure, unerring conviction that God, in his goodness and wisdom, would meet her consent with grace and whatever help that she might need to carry out his will.

Joseph, too, had to overcome his own bewilderment and apprehensions about Mary's unexpected condition. How could it be that his beloved fiancée was already pregnant! Yet in a dream, an angel of the Lord assured him that the child Mary was carrying had been conceived in a way that surpassed nature—"from the Holy Spirit" (Matthew

1:18)—and would "save his people from their sins" (1:21). So Joseph took Mary as his wife. "In this way he showed a readiness of will like Mary's with regard to what God asked of him through the angel" (Pope St. John Paul II, *Guardian of the Redeemer*, 3).

When God unexpectedly singled out this young woman from Nazareth and asked her to play a key role in his plan for Israel's redemption—and that of all humanity—Mary took him at his word and gave herself over to his plan in trust. Her *fiat* was an act of faith in God—faith that allowed God's word to be fulfilled in her and literally become through her the Word made flesh. And this yes to God was not provisional or short-term: it expressed a fundamental and permanent attitude of Mary, repeated over and over in the days and years ahead. The strength of her yes carried her to Bethlehem, pregnant and with no place to deliver her child, and then into Egypt with Joseph and the infant Jesus as they fled to escape the murderous rage of King Herod.

Continually pondering God's word (Luke 2:19, 51), Mary lived in unwavering faith and obedience. Ultimately, she would hold fast on Calvary to the will of the Lord, even in her pain and grief.

What does Mary's assent to God's surprising request demonstrate and model to us?

First, it's okay to question the Lord when something unexpected happens. Mary questioned the angel before saying yes. The angel offered reassurance, not a complete answer to her question. But we shouldn't berate ourselves if we question the Lord when something unexpected happens, especially when it is something we may not have wanted or asked for.

Second, we can better cope with the unexpected—especially if it's not something we wanted—when we live with a sure hope in the goodness of the Lord. Our faith in God's desire for our ultimate good and happiness can carry us through many crises, difficult though they may be.

Third, by responding with trust to the will of the Father, we are able to embrace the unexpected rather than fight it. Mary and Joseph did not know God's exact plan for Jesus or how he would save the world through him. Mysterious though this announcement of the angel was, both Mary and Joseph assented to it and then cooperated with the Lord in carrying it out. Often we waste time and energy rebelling against the unexpected. Consenting to and embracing God's plan—even when this is difficult—gives us peace and the grace and strength to move forward as we watch it unfold in our lives.

With the help and intercession of Mary and Joseph, may we learn to embrace the unexpected surprises of God. As Pope Francis put it so well,

> The Virgin Mary teaches us what it means to live in the Holy Spirit and what it means to accept the news of God in our life. She conceived Jesus by the work of the Holy Spirit, and every Christian, each one of us, is called to accept the Word of God, to accept Jesus inside of us, and then to bring him to everyone. (Regina Caeli Address, April 28, 2013)

Understand!

1. What does Mary's exchange with Gabriel suggest to you about her character and disposition? Note several character traits that stand out to you in Luke's portrait of Mary as the Evangelist's account of this event unfolds.

_____

_____

_____

_____

_____

2. Explain in your own words the significance of Mary's virginity and the importance and implications of the miraculous way in which Jesus was conceived. How does Gabriel describe the action of the Holy Spirit?

_____

_____

_____

_____

_____

3. What, in your opinion, prepared, equipped, and/or enabled Mary to make her response to God in faith and trust?

_____

_____

_____

_____

_____

4. What qualities of Joseph do you note as the narrative in Matthew 1:18-24 progresses? What did the angel tell Joseph about the child Mary was carrying? What is Joseph's role in God's plan for salvation? His role toward Jesus and Mary?

_____

_____

_____

_____

_____

5. List the titles and descriptions of the child to be born that the angels announced to Mary and Joseph. What do you understand by each of these attributions? Which title or name is most meaningful to you at this point in your life? Why?

_____

_____

_____

_____

_____

▶ In the Spotlight
Mary, Model of Total Self-Surrender

The birth of Jesus is the greatest act of love the world has ever seen—God becoming man, one of us. On God's side, this meant three things: that the Father would love us so much that he would send his only Son to be our Savior; that the Son would love us so much that he would lay down his life for us in the cruel suffering of the cross; and that the Holy Spirit would love us so much that he would bring about the incarnation of the Word.

But there also had to be an incredible act of love on the part of mankind to receive God's infinite love and to respond to it appropriately. Mary's loving response at the Annunciation, seen in her act of total self-surrender, was precisely what God awaited. Love is measured by giving, and Mary gave herself completely, unreservedly, and joyfully to God's plan. Mary was completely open to the will of God. In her self-abandonment, she called herself "the handmaid of the Lord," ready to do whatever the Lord would ask of her. She gave her total consent: "Let it be done to me according to your word" (Luke 1:38). This allowed the Holy Spirit to bring forth the fullness of life in Mary in the person of Jesus Christ.

—**Andrew Apostoli, CFR,** *Following Mary to Jesus: Our Lady as Mother, Teacher, and Advocate*

True freedom is found in our loving embrace of the Father's will. From Mary, full of grace, we learn that Christian freedom is more than liberation from sin. . . . It is the freedom to love God and our brothers and sisters with a pure heart, and to live a life of joyful hope for the coming of Christ's kingdom.

—**Pope Francis,** Homily, August 15, 2014

Grow!

1. Choose several adjectives to describe how you think Mary must have felt about her pregnancy. When have you had similar feelings about surprising news?

_____

_____

_____

_____

_____

2. Think of an occasion when you felt that God was asking something unexpected of you or something outside of your comfort zone. What was your response to him in this situation? Fear of what God was asking of you? Reluctance to give up your own plans or desires? What were your questions and your prayers like then? What did you learn about yourself through the experience?

_____

_____

_____

_____

_____

3. What place does the Holy Spirit have in your day-to-day life? Describe some ways that you see the Spirit at work in you and in those around you. How open and responsive are you to the Spirit's action and promptings in your life?

_____

_____

_____

_____

_____

4. How did Mary and Joseph's unwavering trust in God's goodness and plan for their lives help them to embrace their new situation? How can you grow in trust and hope of God's goodness and his desire for your ultimate happiness? Can you foresee something fresh or surprisingly new coming to birth in your present circumstances because of your trust in God and obedience to him?

_____

_____

_____

_____

_____

5. How close do you feel to Mary? What might you do to deepen your relationship with her?

_____

_____

_____

_____

_____

▶ In the Spotlight
Willing to Be Surprised by God

Plenty of other women of the Bible embraced the unexpected. And that's not surprising, because our God is a God of surprises—that's often the way the Holy Spirit works in our lives.

Elizabeth, Mary's cousin, never expected to bear a child in her old age, nor have "the mother of my Lord" (Luke 1:43) come to visit and assist her. Nor would she have expected her husband, Zechariah, to be struck mute until her child was about to be circumcised (1:20, 59-64). And did she ever dare to think that her young son would one day live in the desert and announce the coming of the Messiah?

The elderly widow and prophetess Anna had spent most of her life fasting and praying in the Temple. She probably did not think that she would see the Messiah in her lifetime. But when she spotted the baby Jesus that day, she "began to praise God and to speak about the child to all who were looking for the redemption of Jerusalem" (Luke 2:38).

The Samaritan woman probably thought that by coming to the well in the middle of the day, she would be alone. What a surprise to encounter a Jewish rabbi who would speak to her and know all about her past life! But she embraced the life-giving water he had for her, and ended up as one of the first evangelists.

Mary Magdalene, full of sorrow at the death of her Master, wanted to anoint Jesus' body with spices. She did not expect to find an empty tomb or a man who she at first thought was the gardener call her name. And no one expected that this woman would be the first disciple to witness the resurrection or announce it to the Twelve.

The fact is that we should expect the unexpected, and the more that we live our lives in the power of the Holy Spirit, the more we will be anxious and willing to be surprised by God!

Reflect!

1. Reflect and meditate on these insights from Pope Benedict XVI:

> I consider it important to focus . . . on the final sentence of Luke's annunciation narrative: "And the angel departed from her" (Luke 1:38). The great hour of Mary's encounter with God's messenger—in which her whole life is changed—comes to an end, and she remains there alone, with a task that truly surpasses all human capacity. There are no angels standing round her. She must continue along the path that leads through many dark moments—from Joseph's dismay at her pregnancy to the moment when Jesus is said to be out of his mind (cf. Mark 3:21; John 10:20), right up to the night of the Cross.
>
> How often in these situations must Mary have returned inwardly to the hour when God's angel had spoken to her, pondering afresh the greeting: "Rejoice, full of grace!" and the consoling words: "Do not be afraid!" The angel departs; her mission remains, and with it matures her

inner closeness to God, a closeness that in her heart she is able to see and touch. (*Jesus of Nazareth, The Infancy Narratives*)

2. Reflect on the following Scripture passages that could help you when you face situations—whether anticipated or wholly unexpected—that challenge you to say yes to what the Lord is asking of you:

Sacrifice and offering you do not desire,
   but you have given me an open ear.
Burnt offering and sin offering
   you have not required.
Then I said, "Here I am;
   in the scroll of the book it is written of me.
I delight to do your will, O my God;
   your law is within my heart." (Psalm 40:6-8)

They went to a place called Gethsemane; and [Jesus] said to his disciples, "Sit here while I pray." He took with him Peter and James and John, and began to be distressed and agitated. And he said to them, "I am deeply grieved, even to death; remain here, and keep awake." And going a little farther, he threw himself on the ground and prayed that, if it were possible, the hour might pass from him. He said, "Abba, Father, for you all things are possible; remove this cup from me; yet, not what I want, but what you want." (Mark 14:32-36)

▶ In the Spotlight
A Call within a Call

St. Teresa of Calcutta's life, like Mary's, took a surprising turn when she received an unexpected new calling from the Lord.

Agnes Bojaxhiu was born in Skopje (modern Macedonia) in 1910. She joined the Sisters of Loreto in Ireland at the age of eighteen and, after completing her novitiate, was sent to teach schoolchildren in India. Upon taking her first vows as a nun in 1931, she chose to be named Teresa. In 1944 she was appointed headmistress of the Loreto convent school in Calcutta.

On September 10, 1946, Mother Teresa experienced what she later described as her "inspiration," her "call within a call," while traveling by train to Darjeeling for her annual retreat. "I was to leave the convent and help the poor while living among them," she later wrote.

With approval from Church authorities, Mother Teresa began her missionary work in 1948, replacing her Loreto habit with a simple white cotton sari decorated with a blue border. She adopted Indian citizenship and, after taking basic medical training, ventured into the slums. She had no income and resorted to begging for food and supplies.

Soon several young women joined Sister Teresa in caring for the destitute and starving, and on October 7, 1950, she received Vatican approval to start a new diocesan congregation, the Missionaries of Charity. Its mission was to care for, in her own words, "the hungry, the naked, the homeless, the crippled, the blind, the lepers, all those people who feel unwanted, unloved, uncared for throughout society, people that have become a burden to the society and are shunned by everyone." After serving the "poorest of the poor" for more than forty-five years, Mother Teresa died on September 5, 1997. During her life and in the years after her death, she received countless awards and honors, among them the 1979 Nobel Peace Prize.

Agnes Bojaxhiu truly embraced the unexpected, "the call within a call" that set her life on a remarkable path. Her willing obedience bore great fruit. Today, more than 4,500 Missionaries of Charity serve in 123 countries, caring for sick and abandoned children, the elderly, people with AIDS, refugees, the mentally ill, those suffering from leprosy, and the dying. These services are provided without charge to people, regardless of their religion or social caste.

Mother Teresa of Calcutta was beatified on October 19, 2003, by Pope John Paul II and canonized on September 4, 2016, by Pope Francis.

Act!

This week, take time to intercede for someone who has had something unexpected happen in his or her life recently that is a struggle—perhaps a divorce or separation, a difficult medical diagnosis like cancer, or the sudden death of a loved one. In addition to praying for that person, ask the Lord for ideas of how you can help him or her, maybe with a visit, a phone call, or a meal.

▶ In the Spotlight
Bearers of Christ

Our Lady said yes for the human race. Each one of us must echo that yes for our own lives.

We are all asked if we will surrender what we are, our humanity, our flesh and blood, to the Holy Spirit and allow Christ to fill the emptiness formed by the particular shape of our life.

The surrender that is asked of us includes complete and absolute trust; it must be like Our Lady's surrender, without condition and without reservation.

We shall not be asked to do more than the Mother of God; we shall not be asked to become extraordinary or set apart or to make a hard and fast rule of life or to compile a manual of mortifications or heroic resolutions; we shall not be asked to cultivate our souls like rare hothouse flowers; we shall not, most of us, even be allowed to do that.

What we shall be asked to give is our flesh and blood, our daily life—our thoughts, our service to one another, our affections and loves, our words, our intellect, our waking, working, and sleeping, our ordinary human joys and sorrows—to God.

To surrender all that we are, as we are, to the Spirit of Love in order that our lives may bear Christ into the world—that is what we shall be asked.

Our Lady has made this possible. Her *fiat* was for herself and for us, but if we want God's will to be completed in us as it is in her, we must echo her *fiat*.

—**Caryll Houselander,** *The Reed of God*

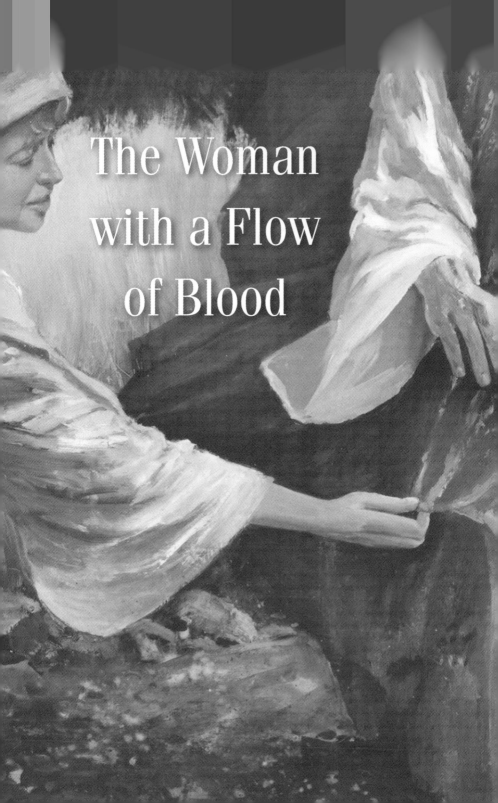

The Woman
with a Flow
of Blood

Mark 5:24-34

⁵:²⁴A large crowd followed [Jesus] and pressed in on him. ²⁵Now there was a woman who had been suffering from hemorrhages for twelve years. ²⁶She had endured much under many physicians, and had spent all that she had; and she was no better, but rather grew worse. ²⁷She had heard about Jesus, and came up behind him in the crowd and touched his cloak, ²⁸for she said, "If I but touch his clothes, I will be made well." ²⁹Immediately her hemorrhage stopped; and she felt in her body that she was healed of her disease. ³⁰Immediately aware that power had gone forth from him, Jesus turned about in the crowd and said, "Who touched my clothes?" ³¹And his disciples said to him, "You see the crowd pressing in on you; how can you say, 'Who touched me?'" ³²He looked all around to see who had done it. ³³But the woman, knowing what had happened to her, came in fear and trembling, fell down before him, and told him the whole truth. ³⁴He said to her, "Daughter, your faith has made you well; go in peace, and be healed of your disease."

> The need to be freed urges her to dare and her faith "snatches," so to speak, healing from the Lord. She who believes "touches" Jesus and draws from him a saving grace.
> —**Pope Francis**, Angelus Address, June 28, 2015

(See also Matthew 9:20-22; Luke 8:43-48.)

Chronic illness can be so devastating—and can make one desperate enough to try anything! Just look at this woman with the flow of blood. For twelve years she had futilely sought a cure for her bleeding disorder, only to be disappointed time and time again (Mark 5:25-26). Who wouldn't have been discouraged, even hopeless, after spending so much money on one doctor after another, only to have gotten worse (5:26)? Yet this woman hadn't given up hope. Moved by expectant faith (and courage), she reached out to Jesus, confident that she would be healed simply by touching his clothes!

It's not clear exactly what physical disorder this woman suffered from, but whatever the cause, her ailment was chronic. In addition to enduring the painful discomfort from such steady bleeding, she probably experienced debilitating anemia, weight loss, and weakness. No medical treatment had relieved her symptoms or cured her.

However, much more than this woman's physical well-being was affected by her condition; she had known years of loneliness, grief, and isolation. According to Mosaic law, a woman was considered "unclean" each month for seven days during the "regular discharge from her body" (Leviticus 15:19). The purpose of this law was not to demean or disparage women; rather, it reflected the high regard the Israelites had for the sacredness of life and for a woman's contact with that sacredness in reproduction. But the nature of the ailment of the woman in this Gospel scene—a continuous flow of blood—would have rendered her constantly impure nonetheless:

> If a woman has a discharge of blood for many days, not at the time of her impurity, or if she has a discharge beyond the time of her impurity, all the days of the discharge she shall continue in uncleanness; as in the days of her impurity, she shall be unclean. Every bed on which she lies during all the days of her discharge shall be treated as the bed of her impurity; and everything on which she sits shall be unclean, as in the uncleanness of her impurity. Whoever touches these things shall be unclean, and shall wash his clothes, and bathe in water, and be unclean until the evening. (Leviticus 15:25-27)

If this woman were relatively young, her condition would have made marriage and childbearing impossible. If she were already married and had borne children before the onset of her disorder, its chronic nature would have severely restricted her relations with her husband and family. Regardless of her age or marital status, her continual "uncleanness" would have curtailed her activities and cut her off from her friends, since any contact with her would have made them ritually unclean too—just touching a cup she had drunk from or a chair she had sat on would "defile" them. Consequently, the afflicted woman could not participate in the social life of her village or in the public worship of God.

Encouraged by reports of how Jesus had already healed so many people (Mark 5:27), this woman dared to hope the same for herself. Emboldened by her belief in Jesus' power, she was determined to reach out to him for help. Just coming in contact with the fringe, or hem, of Jesus' garment would be enough to heal her, she thought (Matthew 9:20; Luke 8:44). "Her desire for connection and healing broke through the fear from isolation and disgrace," noted Anglican priest David Giffen. "She came to experience faith as both a verb and an action, touching Jesus, and asking him to take away her pain." But because she was legally unclean and embarrassed by her illness, she wanted to slip through the crowd and touch Jesus' robe without attracting any attention.

When she touched Jesus' clothing, the woman's bleeding ceased, and she immediately felt that she had been healed (Mark 5:29). After so many years of suffering, she was well; her body was healthy and free of pain, and her hope had been fulfilled! But when she tried to disappear into the noisy throng unnoticed, Jesus gave her away.

Jesus was certain that he hadn't simply been jostled accidentally in the press of the crowd. He'd been touched purposefully by a hand reaching out in eager faith, and he felt energy go out from him (Mark 5:30).

When Jesus asked, "Who touched me?" (5:31), he wanted to know who had drawn upon his power with such firm confidence in him.

The woman must have trembled, ashamed to admit that in her uncleanness she had dared to touch the teacher. Yet she was sure of his mercy, for hadn't he just granted her healing? So falling at his feet, she told "the whole truth" (Mark 5:33). Her story, so long one of repeated disappointments, now culminated in joy and gratitude. She "declared in the presence of all the people why she had touched him, and how she had been immediately healed" (Luke 8:47). In reply, Jesus commended and affirmed her: "Daughter, your faith has made you well; go in peace, and be healed of your disease" (Mark 5:34).

Emboldened by her belief in Jesus' power, she was determined to reach out to him for help.

Not only did Jesus restore this woman's health; he also restored her place in society. When he called the woman to come forth from the crowd to publicly acknowledge her healing, Jesus established her as clean in the eyes of all. By his gracious affirmation of her, she was freed from her "civic death" and given full and abundant life.

The Evangelists don't tell us the name of this woman. Since she remains unnamed, each of us can more easily put ourselves in her place—and follow her example. When we are facing challenges or a crisis, Jesus is eager to answer us with miraculous signs of his presence and love and healing power—but we first have to reach out to him. As Pope Francis declared in an address urging us to be as daring as this woman, "This is faith: to touch Jesus is to draw from him the grace that saves. It saves us, it saves our spiritual life, it saves us from so many problems" (Angelus Address, June 28, 2015). Today God continues to work miracles in our midst to bring us healing, wholeness, and deeper conversion to him.

Understand!

1. What does Mark's description of this woman's condition and of her actions indicate about her? How would you characterize her personality? Her life circumstances? Her faith?

_____

_____

_____

_____

_____

2. Why, in your opinion, did this woman have such faith that Jesus *could heal* and that she *would be healed* if she just touched his cloak? Note that Mark wrote that "she had heard about Jesus" (5:27). What does this suggest about the importance and power of giving testimony? About the importance and power of faith?

_____

_____

_____

_____

_____

3. How would you describe Jesus' response to this woman and his concern for her? Recall a few other examples in the Gospels that recount Jesus' encounters with women and his attitudes toward them.

_____

_____

_____

_____

_____

4. Why did it matter to Jesus who had touched him? From Mark's account of Jesus' encounter with this woman, what insights have you gained into Jesus' human nature? Into Jesus' divine nature?

_____

_____

_____

_____

_____

5. Describe some of the ways in which you think this woman experienced peace because of her healing. What areas of her life were now radically changed? How might her family and friends have been affected by her healing?

_____

_____

_____

_____

_____

▶ In the Spotlight
Jesus' Regard and Care for Women

Jesus' healing of the woman with the hemorrhage is only one of many instances in which he showed concern for women. In fact, Matthew, Mark, and Luke all relate that this encounter occurred while Jesus was on his way to help the daughter of Jairus, a twelve-year-old girl whom he would raise from the dead (Matthew 9:18-25; Mark 5:21-43; Luke 8:40-56).

If we read through the Gospels, paying attention to Jesus' encounters with women, we see that he healed Peter's mother-in-law of a fever (Mark 1:29-31), showed his compassion for the widow of Nain by restoring her only son to life (Luke 7:11-18), and straightened the bent back of a woman who had suffered from her deformity for eighteen years (Luke 13:10-17). He treated the woman caught in adultery with mercy and kindness as he encouraged her to sin no more (John 8:1-11), freed Mary Magdalene from the demonic influences that had plagued her (Luke 8:2), and enjoyed deep friendship with Martha and her sister, Mary (Luke 10:38-42; John 11:1-3; 12:1-3).

Women were among Jesus' most dedicated followers (Luke 8:2-3; Matthew 27:55-56), and it was to them that he first showed himself after the resurrection (Matthew 28:1-10; Mark 16:1-10; Luke 24:1-11; John 20:11-18).

Grow!

1. Of the qualities revealed by the woman in Mark 5:24-34—for example, her faith, courage, hope, or honesty—which do you most admire? Why? How might you model yourself after her, especially when you are in a crisis situation?

_____

_____

_____

_____

_____

2. Do you find it easy or difficult to identify personally with the faith and daring of this woman? Explain. What might hinder you from asking Jesus to meet your personal needs? Shame? Feelings of unworthiness? Fear of being disappointed?

_____

_____

_____

_____

_____

3. Touch is an important means by which humans connect with one another and express love, care, and support—the embrace of a husband and wife, a mother's caress of her child, the warm handshake or hug of a friend. Lack of touch can be isolating. Reaching out to touch another can express longing, need, or hope. A touch can bring healing—or injury. What aspects of touch (or lack of touch) are at play in this story? What has this story taught you about the importance and power of touch?

_____

_____

_____

_____

_____

4. Recall an instance in your life when you recognized that Jesus had healed you physically or spiritually. How had you approached him with this need? What was your reaction to this healing? How did this encounter with Jesus impact your life and/or change you?

_____

_____

_____

_____

_____

5. Jesus called this woman "daughter" and commended her for her faith (Mark 5:34). Have you ever felt that Jesus honored you for putting your faith in him? If so, how did you respond to his

affirmation? Do you identify and recognize yourself as a daughter of God? Why or why not?

_____

_____

_____

_____

_____

▶ In the Spotlight
"Power Had Gone Forth from Him"

The Greek word for "power," *dunamis*, is the root of the word "dynamic." Divine power and dynamism radiated from Jesus and drew people to him: "All in the crowd were trying to touch him, for power came out from him and healed all of them" (Luke 6:19). In confronting sickness, sin, Satan, and even death, Jesus acted with the power and sovereign authority that were his as the Son of God, the Messiah-Redeemer.

When Jesus worked miracles two thousand years ago, he manifested his love and compassion and called men and women to faith in him. His miracles demonstrated his divine mission of redemption and expressed the saving power and mercy of God. Although Jesus manifested mighty power and no doubt made a sensation, he didn't perform miracles to call attention to himself or enhance his reputation. Rather, his deeds communicated the love and compassion of God for his people. He often cured people of their physical ailments while at the same time healing them spiritually by forgiving their sins, freeing them from fear or shame or guilt, and restoring hope.

In particular, regarding the encounter between the woman with a flow of blood and Jesus, biblical scholar George Montague, SM, noted that the account has much to teach us:

Mark sees Jesus as a living dynamo, which, when contacted by faith, inevitably releases power. The woman senses at once that she is healed. Jesus does not allow her to escape anonymously in the crowd but cries out, "Who touched my garments?" The woman comes forward and publicly confesses her action and her gratitude to Jesus. Jesus *then* pronounces the word of healing. This account carries an important teaching: First, healing is a personal encounter with Jesus. It is not a magical or mechanical event, though physical touch may be involved. The healed person must meet Jesus, even if the meeting takes place *after* the healing. Second, a public confession of Jesus is part of the healing process. Others may thus come to faith through this woman's witness. Finally, even though the physical event of her healing has taken place already, Jesus' *word* of healing completes the action. He further personalizes it, and teaches that her touch would have been meaningless without faith. (*Mark: Good News for Hard Times*)

These miraculous events of the Gospels still have something to say to us: they are Jesus' invitation to open ourselves to receive his mercy and to embrace the salvation he came to proclaim to us.

Reflect!

1. St. Ambrose, one of the Church Fathers, wrote, "She touched the hem of his garment, she approached him in a spirit of faith, she believed, and she realized that she was cured. . . . So we too, if we wish to be saved, should reach out in faith to touch the garment of Christ."

Do you have a problem or concern that is so long-standing—like the woman's twelve-year affliction—that you feel discouraged and have little hope of any solution? What pressing need would you bring to Jesus now? Let the story of this woman's healing help you to see in your suffering an opportunity to reach out to Jesus afresh, touching him with faith.

2. Read and prayerfully reflect on the following Scripture passage that illustrates the faith of another woman who did not hesitate to approach Jesus with her need:

> Jesus . . . went away to the district of Tyre and Sidon. Just then a Canaanite woman from that region came out and started shouting, "Have mercy on me, Lord, Son of David; my daughter is tormented by a demon." But he did not answer her at all. And his disciples came and urged him, saying, "Send her away, for she keeps shouting after us." He answered, "I was sent only to the lost sheep of the house of Israel." But she came and knelt before him, saying, "Lord, help me." He answered, "It is not fair to take the children's food and throw it to the dogs." She said, "Yes, Lord, yet even the dogs eat the crumbs that fall from their masters' table." Then Jesus answered her, "Woman, great is your faith! Let it be done for you as you wish." And her daughter was healed instantly. (Matthew 15:21-28)

What similarities do you see between the Canaanite woman's encounter with Jesus and the encounter of the woman with the hemorrhage with Jesus?

▶ In the Spotlight
Jesus Called Her "Daughter"

She is the only woman in Scripture that Jesus addressed as "daughter." He didn't call her "daughter of Abraham" or "daughter of Jerusalem." Neither did he use an honorable yet formal, impersonal title such as "lady" or "woman." Instead, he spoke to the woman afflicted with an issue of blood a word of endearment that describes a personal relationship, a warm, demonstrative term that gives identity as well as public social acceptance. In calling her "daughter," Jesus gave this nameless woman a profoundly meaningful name.

Many Christians have reflected on the significance of Jesus addressing the woman who reached out to him in faith as "daughter." For example, contemporary Scripture commentator George Martin notes, "Jesus addresses her as daughter, a term of affection but also a proclamation that there is a bond between them: Jesus welcomes to himself one who had been cut off from human relationships" (*Bringing the Gospel of Mark to Life: Insight and Inspiration*). Centuries earlier, St. John Chrysostom, one of the ancient Fathers of the Church, wrote in his homilies on the Gospels, "He calls her 'daughter' because she was saved by her faith; for faith in Christ makes us His children."

In her book *The Women of the Passion*, Kathleen Murphy offers these thoughts:

> Desperation had brought her to faith. She was changed forever. Jesus affirmed her as *'Daughter.'* Among the discipleship she was recognized as a daughter of the Church and in consequence her story was preserved for the edification of future generations. As a grateful member of the faith community, it is reasonable to believe that she was among the group of women from Galilee who traveled with him from Galilee to Jerusalem (Mt 27:55).

Adding yet another insight, Ann Spangler and Jean E. Syswerda note in their devotional study *Women of the Bible,*

> Instead of scolding and shaming her, Jesus praised her: "Daughter, your faith has healed you. Go in peace and be freed from your suffering." His words must have been like water breaching a dam, breaking through her isolation, setting her free. He had addressed her not harshly, but tenderly—not as "woman" or "sinner," but rather as *daughter.* She was no longer alone, but part of his family by virtue of her faith.

And as Pope Francis assures us, the Lord looks upon us all as sons and daughters whom he's eager to cure, restore, and redeem:

> It is the voice of the heavenly Father who speaks in Jesus: "Daughter, you are not cursed, you are not excluded, you are my child!" And every time Jesus approaches us, when we go forth from him with faith, we feel this from the Father: "Child, you are my son, you are my daughter! You are healed. I forgive everyone for everything. I heal all people and all things." (Angelus Address, June 28, 2015)

Act!

Visit someone you know who lives with chronic pain, a physical disability, or a long-standing illness. Show them love and compassion by praying with them. Perhaps you could offer to take them to Mass or take them out for coffee or lunch. Be sure to provide a listening ear!

▶ In the Spotlight
Healed, Body and Soul

When Jesus puts his hands on blind eyes, deaf ears, bent backs, paralyzed limbs, the Creator-God is at work through him, not merely patching up the rents in his old creation, but really bringing in the new. It is true that the life he directly gives to broken bodies is natural life: the flesh that grows in leprous places will crumble one day and Lazarus will have to die again. But the Bible never makes a sharp division between physical and spiritual healing, any more than we can today with our awareness of our psychosomatic unity. When Christ heals, then and now, he heals the whole person, because the whole person stands open to God's re-creative power.

—**Maria Boulding,** *Prayer: Our Journey Home*

The Evangelist Mark presents to us the account of two miraculous cures which Jesus worked for two women: the daughter of one of the elders of the synagogue whose name was Jairus, and a woman who was suffering from a hemorrhage (cf. Mark 5:21-43). These two episodes can be interpreted at two levels: the purely physical—Jesus bends over human suffering and heals the body, and the spiritual level—Jesus came to heal human hearts, to give salvation, and asks for faith in him.

In the first episode, in fact, on hearing that Jairus' little daughter was dead, Jesus tells the ruler of the synagogue, "Do not fear, only believe" (verse 36). He takes the child's father with him to the room where the child is lying and exclaims, "Little girl, I say to you, arise" (verse 41). And she rose and walked.

St. Jerome commented on these words, underlining Jesus' saving power: "Little girl, stand up for my sake, not for your own merit but for my grace. Therefore get up for me: being healed does not depend on your own virtues" (*Homily on the Gospel according to Mark,* 3).

The second episode, that of the woman with the hemorrhage, highlights once again that Jesus came to save the human being in his totality. Indeed, the miracle takes place in two phases: first comes the physical healing, but this is closely linked with the deeper healing, the healing which God's grace gives to those who open themselves to him with faith. Jesus says to the woman: "Daughter, your faith has made you well; go in peace, and be healed of your disease" (Mark 5:34).

These two stories of healing invite us to go beyond a purely horizontal and materialistic vision of life. We ask God to heal so many problems, our practical needs, and this is right, but what we must ask him for insistently is an ever firmer faith, so that the Lord may renew our life, as well as firm trust in his love, in his Providence that never abandons us.

—**Pope Benedict XVI,** Angelus Address, July 1, 2012

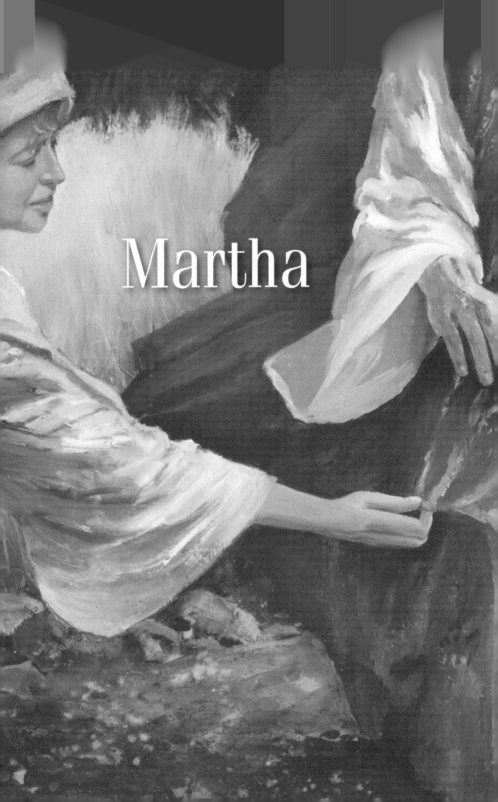

Martha

Luke 10:38-42

^{10:38}Now as they went on their way, [Jesus] entered a certain village, where a woman named Martha welcomed him into her home. ³⁹She had a sister named Mary, who sat at the Lord's feet and listened to what he was saying. ⁴⁰But Martha was distracted by her many tasks; so she came to him and asked, "Lord, do you not care that my sister has left me to do all the work by myself? Tell her then to help me." ⁴¹But the Lord answered her, "Martha, Martha, you are worried and distracted by many things; ⁴²there is need of only one thing. Mary has chosen the better part, which will not be taken away from her."

> **M**artha offers a warmly human portrait of what it means to have Jesus as a friend, allowing him to stretch her faith, rebuke her small vision of the world, and show her what the power of God can do.
> —**Ann Spangler and Jean E. Syswerda,** *Women of the Bible*

John 11:1-6, 20-27; 12:1-3

^{11:1}Now a certain man was ill, Lazarus of Bethany, the village of Mary and her sister Martha. ²Mary was the one who anointed the Lord with perfume and wiped his feet with her hair; her brother Lazarus was ill. ³So the sisters sent a message to Jesus, "Lord, he whom you love is ill." ⁴But when Jesus heard it, he said, "This illness does not lead to death; rather it is for God's glory, so that the Son of God may be glorified through it." ⁵Accordingly, though Jesus loved Martha and her sister and Lazarus, ⁶after having heard that Lazarus was ill, he stayed two days longer in the place where he was. . . . ²⁰When Martha heard that Jesus was coming, she went and met him, while Mary stayed at home. ²¹Martha said to Jesus, "Lord, if you had been here, my brother would not have died. ²²But even now I know that

God will give you whatever you ask of him." [23]Jesus said to her, "Your brother will rise again." [24]Martha said to him, "I know that he will rise again in the resurrection on the last day." [25]Jesus said to her, "I am the resurrection and the life. Those who believe in me, even though they die, will live, [26]and everyone who lives and believes in me will never die. Do you believe this?" [27]She said to him, "Yes, Lord, I believe that you are the Messiah, the Son of God, the one coming into the world."

[12:1]Six days before the Passover Jesus came to Bethany, the home of Lazarus, whom he had raised from the dead. [2]There they gave a dinner for him. Martha served, and Lazarus was one of those at the table with him. [3]Mary took a pound of costly perfume made of pure nard, anointed Jesus' feet, and wiped them with her hair. The house was filled with the fragrance of the perfume.

Martha was a dear friend of Jesus, who frequently visited the home in Bethany that she shared with her siblings, Mary and Lazarus. There Jesus found a restful haven, a place where he could be refreshed from his busy days of teaching and ministering to the crowds that so avidly followed him.

Martha received Jesus with open arms and then got on with the work of hosting him. Hospitality is highly regarded in Middle Eastern culture, so it's natural that she wanted to serve Jesus well. Martha loved Jesus deeply and expressed this love concretely by preparing him a fine meal.

The way Martha welcomed and cared for Jesus shows her recognition of his humanity. Her warmth and hospitality met Jesus' human needs for nourishment, refreshment, and rest. Moreover, Martha's welcome meant not just preparing food and lodging for Jesus and his crowd of apostles. It also expressed her acceptance of Jesus' mission and her desire to contribute to it. However, Martha lost sight of the Lord as she bustled about busily. She was a hospitable but harried hostess, so occupied with serving her guest that she couldn't take the time to sit down with him. When Martha indignantly asked, "Lord, do you not care that my sister has left me to do all the work by myself?" (Luke 10:40), she showed a self-concern that robbed her of the ability to appreciate the precious gift of the moment—fellowship with Jesus.

In her complaint, we find the same Greek verb, *melei*, that the disciples used in their accusation of Jesus during the storm at sea: "Do you not care that we are perishing?" (Mark 4:38). Jesus responded the same way to both upheavals: he calmed the troubled hearts and storms that swept around him. Jesus gently reproached Martha: "You are worried and distracted by many things" (Luke 10:41). Other English translations of the original Greek text call her "troubled," "anxious," "fretting and fussing," "upset over all these details," and "bothered about providing so many things."

> Jesus pointed Martha in the right direction, helping her to unify her life and prioritize her concerns.

Did Martha resent having to serve alone because she felt that Mary was being lazy? Perhaps she was comparing herself to Mary or was a bit jealous of her sister comfortably sitting at their guest's feet. But no matter what Martha's anxieties and worries were, she had a profound love for Jesus; she was at ease with him, comfortable and secure in his love and in her friendship with him. She knew where to go when she was upset and needed help—to Jesus—and he pointed her in the right direction, helping her to unify her life and prioritize her concerns.

Jesus' response to Martha wasn't a harsh reproof. He knew that her solicitude was genuine, that she was translating her love for him into hospitable acts. Jesus appreciated Martha's loving labor and recognized the generosity of her bustling nature, but he urged her to relax and enjoy his company. His reply was meant to help Martha recognize how senseless and unnecessary her anxieties were. "There is need of only one thing" (Luke 10:42). Or as the *Living Bible* translation reads, "There is really only one thing worth being concerned about."

We may feel sorry for Martha, left to fix the dinner alone, and begrudge Mary her "better part" at the feet of Jesus. But rather than seeing the postures of the two sisters as mutually exclusive—the active life of service versus the contemplative life of prayer—we should recognize in Martha and Mary complementary aspects of the call given to all followers of Christ. As Scripture commentator Stephen J. Binz has noted,

> In affirming the choice of Mary, we may feel that Martha's hospitality and service are devalued. Yet, when Jesus highlighted the one thing necessary, he did not mean that everything else has no importance. These sisters are not caricatures of two opposing choices, one of which must be selected over the other. This is not a contrast between a fussy, argumentative busybody and her tranquil, attentive sister. Rather, the sisters express two interdependent aspects of discipleship, both of which are necessary. Hearing the Word and doing it are both essential and complementary facets of following Jesus. There is a time to listen and a time to act. (*Women of the Gospels: Friends and Disciples of Jesus*)

Indeed, in each of our lives, there's a time to listen, to pray, and to sit at Jesus' feet, and there's a time to act, to serve, and to wash the feet of those whom the Lord gives us. By balancing action and contemplation in a creative tension in our own lives, we make concrete our love for Jesus. "Be both Martha and Mary. Diligently carry out your duties, and often recollect yourself and put yourself in spirit at the feet of our Lord," St. Francis de Sales wrote in a letter to a married woman seeking spiritual guidance. "Say, 'My Lord, whether I'm rushing around or staying still, I am all yours and you are all mine. You are my first spouse, and whatever I do is for love of you'" (*Letters to Persons in the World*).

John the Evangelist gives us a later view of Martha, again free and bold in her friendship with Jesus, as she lamented to him, "Lord, if you had been here, my brother would not have died. But even now I know that God will give you whatever you ask of him" (John 11:21-22). Assured by Jesus that Lazarus—and anyone who believes in him—will rise again, Martha made an amazing declaration of faith in him: "Yes, Lord, I believe that you are the Messiah, the Son of God, the one coming into the world" (11:27).

John's Gospel (12:1-3) also gives us the final scene in which we again see Martha and Mary in their familiar places:

> Six days before the Passover Jesus came to Bethany, the home of Lazarus, whom he had raised from the dead. There they gave a dinner for him. Martha served, and Lazarus was one of those at the table with him. Mary took a pound of costly perfume made of pure nard, anointed Jesus' feet, and wiped them with her hair. The house was filled with the fragrance of the perfume.

Once again Martha is serving and Mary is at the Lord's feet. Might we think that Martha had learned her lesson well earlier and is now joyful, content, and wholehearted in her loving service, enjoying the fragrance of her sister's act? Does not each sister delight in honoring their beloved friend in her own way?

Understand!

1. Consider the way in which each of the two sisters welcomed Jesus into their home. What similarities would you note in Martha's and Mary's responses to Jesus when he visited them? What differences?

_____

_____

_____

_____

_____

2. What does the account in Luke 10:38-42 suggest to you about Martha's character and personality? What do the scenes from John 11:1-45 and John 12:1-3 add to your view of her? Which of Martha's character traits do you most admire? Why?

_____

_____

_____

_____

_____

3. What, in your opinion, was Martha's chief motivation in serving Jesus? The main reason for the complaint Martha made to Jesus (Luke 10:40)?

_____

_____

_____

_____

_____

4. What does Jesus' reply to Martha's complaint in Luke 10:41-42 reveal about him? About his outlook toward others and his concern for them? In what tone of voice do you think Jesus replied to Martha? Does Jesus' reply indicate what is at the heart of Martha's fretting and her vexation with Mary? Explain your answer.

_____

_____

_____

_____

_____

5. Martha was free to be very open and honest with Jesus, not hiding her feelings. In your own words, describe Martha's relationship with Jesus. Do you think Martha should have complained directly to her sister rather than to Jesus? Why or why not? Do you think Martha was too forthright and brash with Jesus when she reproached him at Lazarus' tomb (John 11:21)? Why or why not?

_____

_____

_____

_____

_____

▶ In the Spotlight
Bethany

The home of Jesus' beloved friends Martha, Mary, and their brother, Lazarus, was in Bethany (John 11:1), a village located on the eastern slope of the Mount of Olives about three kilometers from Jerusalem on the road to Jericho.

During the last days of his life when Jesus taught daily in the Temple, he was unable to spend the night in Jerusalem because of the plots of the Pharisees. So he withdrew to Bethany (Matthew 21:17; Mark 11:11, 18-19)—most probably to the house of his dear friends. It was here that Martha served Jesus while Mary sat at his feet, listening to his words (Luke 10:38-42). Their home was a haven where he found rest and refreshment in its loving atmosphere, a place of friendship and hospitality. Here too in Bethany, Jesus raised Lazarus from the dead (John 11:1-44), and soon afterwards a feast was celebrated in Lazarus' home at which his sister Mary anointed the feet of Jesus with costly ointment (12:1-8). The Gospel of Luke identifies Bethany as the site of Jesus' ascension into heaven (24:50).

Most likely the village was originally inhabited by the tribe of Benjamin after their return to Palestine from exile in Babylon. The Hebrew word for "house" is *beth*, and the name Bethany may stand for "the house of Ananiah"—the name of one of the Benjamites (cf. Nehemiah 11:32). However, some scholars think Bethany may derive from "Beth-hine," or "the house of dates."

During the Byzantine Empire, Bethany was given the name "El-Azariya"—a corruption of the Greek name "Lazareion." Eusebius of Caesarea, a Greek Church historian, reported that in the fourth century, there was a tomb in the village reputed to be that of Lazarus. A Christian settlement developed there, and archaeologists have established that the area was used as a cemetery in the first century AD, with tombs of this period found a short distance from the church. But while the *Catholic Encyclopedia* notes that the identification of any particular cave as the actual tomb of Lazarus is "merely possible; it has no strong intrinsic or extrinsic authority," there is "every reason to believe that it was in this general location."

Over the following centuries, several Christian churches were successively built near what early tradition held to be Lazarus' burial cave. In the sixteenth century, Moslems built a mosque at the site of the tomb and barred Christians from gaining access to it. But in 1613 the *custos* [Catholic custodians] of the Holy Land obtained permission to build a second entrance to the tomb.

The Roman Catholic Church of St. Lazarus was built in 1952–54 over the ruins of former Byzantine and Crusader-era churches, some remnants of which still survive within this newest building. Beside the church is the reputed tomb of Lazarus, a small chamber built of large hewn stones and originally closed by another stone. A flight of uneven rock-cut steps lead down from the street level to the chamber, and pilgrims today can enter it through the entrance built by the Christians in the seventeenth century, a gate only four feet high and two feet four inches wide. The earlier entrance passage constructed by the Moslems was walled up centuries ago.

The Arab population of the area still calls the village of Bethany "El-Azariya," and the site traditionally known as Lazarus' tomb is venerated by Christians and Moslems alike.

Grow!

1. Imagine how you would go about welcoming Jesus into your home as a guest. What would be your main concern? What would you do to prepare for his visit? Clean house? Cook a meal? Put on a nice outfit? Try to slow down and quiet your spirit?

   _____

   _____

   _____

   _____

   _____

2. Read these Scripture passages about hospitality: Genesis 18:1-8; Romans 12:13; 1 Timothy 5:10; Hebrews 13:2; 1 Peter 4:9. How do you practice hospitality and use your gifts and home to serve

others? Have you ever thrown a party and been so preoccupied with replenishing the table of hors d'oeuvres and keeping the punch bowl filled that you ignored your guests and missed out on enjoying their company?

_____

_____

_____

_____

_____

3. In what areas of your life are you distracted or preoccupied? Why? Is there anything that you are currently worried about? What might you do to find peace and freedom from your anxiety?

_____

_____

_____

_____

_____

4. What "complaints" about your life would you bring to Jesus right now? Be honest with Jesus—and with yourself! How do you think Jesus would respond to you? What help would you like him to offer you?

_____

_____

_____

_____

_____

5. Ask the Holy Spirit to help you take a close look at your own priorities and schedule. Do you put the Lord first, or do you

relegate him to "second place"? How might you make more time and space for Jesus in your life? Should you cut out any "good" but needless activities (or attitudes!) that tend to make you overly busy or anxious like Martha?

_____

_____

_____

_____

_____

▶ In the Spotlight
The Gift of Hospitality

While not everyone feels comfortable at the helm of a social event, some folks have a natural talent for making guests feel special. You might think those hospitality genes are inherited, but that's a myth. Hospitality takes on added dimensions and new definitions when seen through the lens of Christianity.

Some Christians possess hospitality as a spiritual gift. The Bible tells us that every believer is given at least one spiritual gift for the purpose of building up God's church and serving the body of Christ. In other words, our gifts are given not for our own benefit, but for the enrichment of others. We should be serving those around us, including the body of believers, family and friends.

Romans 12:13, however, encourages us all to practice hospitality, whether it is our spiritual gift or not. In fact, the Greek word *philozenia* is actually a combination of two words—*philos*, meaning "affection" and *zenos*, meaning "stranger." While usually translated to mean hospitality, *philozenia* signifies affection toward strangers.

> Above all, maintain an intense love for each other, since love covers a multitude of sins. Be hospitable to one

another without complaining. Based on the gift each one has received, use it to serve others, as good managers of the varied grace of God. (1 Peter 4:8-10)

St. Benedict upheld that "hospitality maintains a prominence in the living (Christian) tradition. . . . The guest represents Christ and has a claim on the welcome and care of the community." In other words, if we love one another, God abides in us and His love is perfected within us and is showered on those with whom we come in contact.

The Book of 1 John makes it plain that when we love others, we are showing our love for God. He loves us completely and unconditionally. Equally, when we love and serve others in the community through hospitality, we are also serving God.

Whether we have the spiritual gift of hospitality or not, it can be a part of our way of life.

—**Kathy Chapman Sharp,** *How to Change the World with Christian Hospitality*

Reflect!

1. Reflect on the warm human portrait that the Evangelist Luke has drawn of Martha and Jesus' friendship with one another.

   Do you feel trusting of Jesus, confident and comfortable enough in his love for you to call him "friend"? How might you deepen your friendship with Jesus?

2. Read and meditate on the following quotation and Scripture passages about friendship:

   A friend is one that knows you as you are, understands where you have been, accepts what you have become, and still, gently allows you to grow. (Anonymous, though often wrongly attributed to Shakespeare.)

The Lord used to speak to Moses face to face, as one speaks to a friend. (Exodus 33:11)

[Jesus said:] "This is my commandment, that you love one another as I have loved you. No one has greater love than this, to lay down one's life for one's friends. You are my friends if you do what I command you. I do not call you servants any longer, because the servant does not know what the master is doing; but I have called you friends, because I have made known to you everything that I have heard from my Father. You did not choose me but I chose you. And I appointed you to go and bear fruit, fruit that will last, so that the Father will give you whatever you ask him in my name. I am giving you these commands so that you may love one another." (John 15:12-17)

▶ In the Spotlight
Welcoming Jesus

Martha welcoming the Lord into her house shows an immediate realization of his humanity. We could say that Martha comprehends all the concrete reality and historicity of the Incarnation: this Jesus is a man and men have their needs. Human beings live surrounded by many cares, many necessities, many problems, which also surface in the deep relationship of friendship.

Jesus is true man and that is just how Martha welcomes him. She allows herself to be involved in the experience of the Incarnation in a very real way.

For Mary, on the other hand, it is not that she does not see the humanity of the Word. It is not the first time that Jesus has entered his friends' house and it is one of his oases of consolation and peace. But what Mary is able to grasp is the realization that Jesus is the Word of God and that to welcome him means therefore welcoming the Word, God's Word. That is why her attitude is one of listening: "Speak, Lord, your servant is listening."

It is clear that these two are not opposed, they do not negate one another. No one can say: I take my stand with Mary; or I stand by Martha. Both of them together tell us in very impressive fashion something precisely on the lines of the friendship, love, intimacy with which we should greet the Lord.

In our house there is room for Martha and room for Mary and we must occupy both places. We must be Mary because we are welcoming the Word; and we must be Martha because we are receiving the Son of man, the Word who became incarnate precisely in order to share the human condition, and from within it to save humanity and the world. . . . The house is one and Mary's task and Martha's are not alternatives, but dispositions which give full realization to the welcome that should be made to Jesus.
—**Cardinal Anastasio Ballestrero**, *Martha and Mary: Meeting Christ as Friend*

Act!

Take both Martha and Mary as models for your life this week. Offer hospitality to someone, making your home a place of welcome. Invite a co-worker or neighbor to dinner, or offer your home as a meeting place for a neighborhood Bible study or children's playgroup. But also take time—*make* time—to "sit at the feet of the Lord": go to Eucharistic Adoration in your parish church, or quietly read and pray over the Mass readings at home before you attend Mass this Sunday.

▶ In the Spotlight
Getting Our Priorities Right

Work and prayer are both important. It is more a question of which of the two should come first. The Gospel is telling us that it is prayer that should come first so that our work will have the guidance and inspiration from God. A quotation says, "When man works, it is only man who works. But when man prays, God works." This reminds us of the Scripture passage, *"If the Lord does not build the house, in vain does the work-man labor; if the Lord does not watch over the city, in vain does the watchman keep vigil"* [cf. Psalm 127:1]. Jesus said, *"I am the vine, you are the branches. Apart from me, you can do nothing"* [cf. John 15:5]. Ultimately, it is God who makes things possible, who makes our work fruitful.

There is a story about two woodcutters. The first woodcutter works eight hours a day. The second works only for five hours. But both of them have equal number of logs cut with their axe. Asked about the secret of his productivity, the second wood-cutter said, "It is because I take time to rest and recharge my body. And while resting, I sharpen my axe."

Nowadays, people have to be reminded of this lesson. Too many among us have the disease called STD—stress, tension, and depression. We work so hard to make ends meet. We rush to meet deadlines, to catch the train, and to come on time for our appointments. At the end of the day, we are exhausted, wasted, dull, and empty. And this happens every day for years. It is summer time, vacation time. But many consider taking vacation as luxury. It has become too expensive, and we can-not even think of taking some time off from work. Worst of all, many of us say that we have no time even to go to Church or to pray. We are just too busy. The Lord is now telling us: "Mar-tha, Martha, you are so worried and anxious about so many things! Relax. Come to me, and I will give you rest!" [cf. Luke

10:41; Matthew 11:28]. We need to come to Jesus to get some rest and lots of sharpening.

Remember: Jesus is the tree; we are the branches. A branch cannot bear fruit if it is not connected to the tree. We are powerless and lifeless if we are not connected to Jesus. We have lots of work to do and many obligations to fulfill. Yes, we have to work hard. But first, let us make sure we find time to sit down at the feet of Jesus and listen to his words, be inspired by his spirit and be strengthened by his grace. Then the work becomes light, the fruits of our labors become sweet and abundant. Let us take home the motto of Saint Benedict: *"Ora et labora."* Pray and work. Not vice versa.

—**Fr. Mike Lagrimas,** Homily, July 16, 2010

Practical Pointers for Bible Discussion Groups

Bible discussion group is another key that can help us unlock God's word. Participating in a discussion or study group—whether through a parish, a prayer group, or a neighborhood—offers us the opportunity to grow not only in our love for God's word but also in our love for one another. We don't have to be trained Scripture scholars to benefit from discussing and studying the Bible together. Bible-study groups provide environments in which we can worship and pray together and strengthen our relationships with other Christians. The following guidelines can help a group get started and run smoothly.

Getting Started

- Decide on a regular time and place to meet. Meeting on a regular basis allows the group to maintain continuity without losing momentum from the previous discussion.

- Set a time limit for each session. An hour and a half is a reasonable length of time in which to have a rewarding discussion on the material contained in each of the sessions in this guide. However, the group may find that a longer time is even more advantageous. If it is necessary to limit the meeting to an hour, select sections of the material that are of greatest interest to the group.

- Designate a moderator or facilitator to lead the discussions and keep the meetings on schedule. This person's role is to help preserve good group dynamics by keeping the discussion on track. He or she should help ensure that no one monopolizes the session and that each person—including the shyest or quietest individual—is offered an opportunity to speak. The group may want to ask members to take turns moderating the sessions.

- Provide enough copies of the study guide for each member of the group, and ask everyone to bring a Bible to the meetings. Each session's Scripture text and related passages for reflection are printed in full in the guides, but you will find that a Bible is helpful for looking up other passages and cross-references. The translation provided in this guide is the New Revised Standard Version Bible: Catholic edition. You may also want to refer to other translations—for example, the New American Bible or the New Jerusalem Bible—to gain additional insights into the text.

- Try to stay faithful to your commitment and attend as many sessions as possible. Not only does regular participation provide coherence and consistency to the group discussions, but it also demonstrates that members value one another and are committed to sharing their lives with one another.

Session Dynamics

- Read the material for each session in advance and take time to consider the questions and your answers to them. The single most important key to any successful Bible study is having everyone prepared to participate.

- As a courtesy to all members of your group, try to begin and end each session on schedule. Being prompt respects the other commitments of the members and allows enough time for discussion. If the group still has more to discuss at the end of the allotted time, consider continuing the discussion at the next meeting.

- Open the sessions with prayer. A different person could have the responsibility of leading the opening prayer at each session. The prayer could be a spontaneous one, a traditional prayer such as the Our Father, or one that relates to the topic of that particular meeting. The members of the group might also want to begin some of the meetings with a song or hymn. Whatever you choose, ask the Holy Spirit to guide your discussion and study of the Scripture text presented in that session.

- Contribute actively to the discussion. Let the members of the group get to know you, but try to stick to the topic so that you won't divert the discussion from its purpose. And resist the temptation to monopolize the conversation so that everyone will have an opportunity to learn from one another.

- Listen attentively to everyone in the group. Show respect for the other members and their contributions. Encourage, support, and affirm them as they share. Remember that many questions have more than one answer and that the experience of everyone in the group can be enriched by considering a variety of viewpoints.

- If you disagree with someone's observation or answer to a question, do so gently and respectfully, in a way that shows that you value the person who made the comment, and then explain your own point of view. For example, rather than saying, "You're wrong!" or "That's ridiculous!" try something like "I think I see what you're getting at, but I think that Jesus was saying something different in this passage." Be careful to avoid sounding aggressive or argumentative. Then, watch to see how the subsequent discussion unfolds. Who knows? You may come away with a new and deeper perspective.

- Don't be afraid of pauses and reflective moments of silence during the session. People may need some time to think about a question before putting their thoughts into words.

- Maintain and respect confidentiality within the group. Safeguard the privacy and dignity of each member by not repeating what has been shared during the discussion session unless you have been given permission to do so. That way everyone will get the greatest benefit out of the group by feeling comfortable enough to share on a deep, personal level.

- End the session with prayer. Thank God for what you have learned through the discussion, and ask him to help you integrate it into your life.

The Lord blesses all our efforts to come closer to him. As you spend time preparing for and meeting with your small group, be confident in the knowledge that Christ will fill you with wisdom, insight, and grace and the ability to see him at work in your daily life.

Sources and Acknowledgments

Introduction: Meeting Crises with Faith and Trust

The Oxford American Dictionary and Language Guide (New York, NY: Oxford University Press, 1999), 225.

Session 1: Shiphrah and Puah

Stephen J. Binz, *The God of Freedom and Life: A Commentary on the Book of Exodus* (Collegeville, MN: The Liturgical Press, 1993), 14.

Ibid.

Benedict XVI, Address to the Pontifical Acaemy, February 27, 2006, http://w2.vatican.va/content/benedict-xvi/en/speeches/2006/february/documents/hf_ben-xvi_spe_20060227_embrione-umano.html.

Rosa Parks, www.biographyonline.net/humanitarian/rosa-parks.html.

George Bush, https://georgewbush-whitehouse.archives.gov/news/releases/2005/12/text/20051201-1.html.

USCCB Intercessory Prayers, http://www.usccb.org/about/pro-life-activities/prayers/intercessory-prayers-for-life.cfm.

Francis, Inaugural Homily, March 19, 2013, http://
w2.vatican.va/content/francesco/en/homilies/2013/docu-
ments/papa-francesco_20130319_omelia-inizio-pontificato.
html.

Session 2: Naomi and Ruth

Kevin Perrotta, *Love Crosses Boundaries: Jonah/Ruth* (Chi-
cago: Loyola Press, 2000), 30.

John Piper, http://www.desiringgod.org/series/
ruth-sweet-bitter-providence/messages

Wendy Beckett, *Sister Wendy's Bible Treasury* (Maryknoll,
NY: Orbis Books, 2012), 65.

Kevin Perrotta, *Prayer, Fasting, and Almsgiving: Spiritual
Practices That Draw Us Closer to God* (Frederick, MD: The
Word Among Us Press, 2012), 27.

The Word Among Us, August 2015, 41.

Anne Costa, *Lord, I Hurt! The Grace of Forgiveness and the
Road to Healing* (Frederick, MD: The Word Among Us Press,
2012), 131.

Dorothy Day, "Notes by the Way," *The Catholic Worker*,
November 1945, 2, http://www.catholicworker.org/dorothy-
day/articles/461.html.

Session 3: Hannah

Craig Morrison, O Carm, "Praying to the God Who 'Remembers'," *The Word Among Us,* August 2010, 53.

Ibid.

Heidi Bratton, *Finding God's Peace in Everyday Challenges* (Frederick, MD: The Word Among Us Press, 2015), 56–57.

Anne Costa, *Breaking into Joy: Meditations for Living in the Love of Christ* (Frederick, MD: The Word Among Us Press, 2014), 116–117.

Alice Camille, *God's Word Today,* March 2007, 21.

Irene Nowell, *Women in the Old Testament* (Collegeville, MN: The Liturgical Press, 1997), 97.

Damasus Winzen, *Pathways in Scripture* (Ann Arbor, MI: Servant Books, 1976), 110.

Jean-Pierre Prévost, *God's Word Today,* February 2007, 13.

George T. Montague, SM, *Mary's Life in the Spirit: Meditations on a Holy Duet* (Frederick, MD: The Word Among Us Press, 2011), 21–22.

Session 4: Mary

Judith Dupré, *Full of Grace: Encountering Mary in Faith, Art, and Life* (New York: Random House, 2010), 53.

Francis, Angelus Address, December 21, 2014, http://
w2.vatican.va/content/francesco/en/angelus/2014/documents/
papa-francesco_angelus_20141221.html.

John Paul II, Guardian of the Redeemer, no. 3, http://
w2.vatican.va/content/john-paul-ii/en/apost_exhortations/
documents/hf_jp-ii_exh_15081989_redemptoris-custos.html.

Francis, Regina Caeli Address, April 28, 2013, http://
w2.vatican.va/content/francesco/en/angelus/2013/documents/
papa-francesco_regina-coeli_20130428.html.

Andrew Apostoli, CFR, *Following Mary to Jesus: Our Lady
as Mother, Teacher, and Advocate* (Ijamsville, MD: The Word
Among Us Press, 2009), 18.

Francis, Homily, August 15, 2014, http://w2.vatican.va/
content/francesco/en/homilies/2014/documents/papa-fran-
cesco_20140815_corea-omelia-assunzione.html.

Joseph Ratzinger/Benedict XVI, *Jesus of Nazareth, The
Infancy Narratives* (New York: Image/Random House, Inc.,
2012), 37–38.

Caryll Houselander, *The Reed of God* (Allen, Texas: Christian Classics, Inc., 1996), 11-13. Copyright © 1944 by Caryll
Houselander.

Session 5: The Woman with a Flow of Blood

Francis, Angelus Address, June 28, 2015, http://w2.vatican.
va/content/francesco/en/angelus/2015/documents/papa-fran-
cesco_angelus_20150628.html.

David Giffen, Homily, http://www.stpaulscathedral.on.ca/worship/homilies/davidgiffen/Pentecost%20IV%20Homily.pdf.

Francis, Angelus Address, June 28, 2015, http://w2.vatican.va/content/francesco/en/angelus/2015/documents/papa-francesco_angelus_20150628.html.

George T. Montague, SM, *Mark: Good News for Hard Times* (Ann Arbor, MI: Servant Books, 1981), 68.

Ambrose, *Expositio Evangelii sec. Lucam,* VI, 56, 58, quoted in *The Navarre Bible: The Gospel of Saint Mark,* with a commentary by the members of the Faculty of Theology of the University of Navarre (Blackrock, Ireland: Four Courts Press, 1992), 101.

George Martin, *Bringing the Gospel of Mark to Life: Insight and Inspiration* (Ijamsville, MD: The Word Among Us Press, 2007), 119.

John Chrysostom, *Vict. Ant. e Cat. in Marc.; Hom. in Matt.,* 31, http://www.ccel.org/ccel/aquinas/catena2.iii.v.html.

Kathleen M. Murphy, *The Women of the Passion* (Liguori, MO: Liguori, 2007), 68.

Ann Spangler and Jean E. Syswerda, *Women of the Bible: A One-Year Devotional Study of Women in Scripture* (Grand Rapids, MI: Zondervan Publishing House, 1999), 334.

Francis, Angelus Address, June 28, 2015, http://w2.vatican.va/content/francesco/en/angelus/2015/documents/papa-francesco_angelus_20150628.html.

Maria Boulding, *Prayer: Our Journey Home* (Ann Arbor, MI: Servant Books, 1980), 65.

Benedict XVI, Angelus Address, July 1, 2012, http://w2.vatican.va/content/benedict-xvi/en/angelus/2012/documents/hf_ben-xvi_ang_20120701.html.

Session 6: Martha

Ann Spangler and Jean E. Syswerda, *Women of the Bible: A One-Year Devotional Study of Women in Scripture* (Grand Rapids, MI: Zondervan Publishing House, 1999), 366.

Stephen J. Binz, *Women of the Gospels: Friends and Disciples of Jesus* (Grand Rapids, MI: Brazos Press, 2011), 88.

Francis de Sales, *Letters to Persons in the World*, quoted in *Live Jesus! Wisdom from Saints Francis de Sales and Jane de Chantal*, ed. Louise Perrotta (Ijamsville, MD: The Word Among Us Press, 2000), 52.

Kathy Chapman Sharp, *How to Change the World with Christian Hospitality,* http://www.lifeway.com/Article/Christian-Hospitality. E-mail: kathy@kathychapmansharp.com. Used with permission.

"Bethany," Catholic Encyclopedia, https://en.wikisource.org/wiki/Catholic_Encyclopedia_(1913)/Bethany.

Anastasio Ballestrero, *Martha and Mary: Meeting Christ as Friend* (Middleton, Slough, UK: St. Pauls, 1994), 38–39.

Mike Lagrimas, Homily, http://katoliko .org/2010/07/16/16th-sunday-in-ordinary-time/. Used with permission of the author.

The Word Among Us
Keys to the Bible Series
For Individuals or Groups

These studies open up the meaning of the Scriptures while placing each passage within the context of the Bible and Church tradition.

Each of the six sessions feature

- The Scripture text to be studied and insightful commentary
- Questions for reflection, discussion, and personal application
- "In the Spotlight" sections that offer wisdom from the saints, personal testimony, and fascinating historical background

Here are just a few of our popular titles:

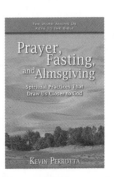

Treasures Uncovered: The Parables of Jesus

Prayer, Fasting, and Almsgiving

Embracing God's Plan for Marriage

The Psalms: Gateway to Prayer

Check out all the studies available in this series
by going online at **bookstore.wau.org**
or
call Customer Service at **1-800-775-9673**